A TIME TO REBOOT

SHARON ALLEN

To Melody,
Love,
Sharon

This is a work of fiction. All of the characters, names, incidents, organizations, and dialogue in this novel are either the products of the author's imagination or are used fictitiously.

ISBN: 10:1502820730
ISBN-13:978-1502820730

DEDICATION

I'm dedicating this book to one of the best friends in my world, Glenice Ashton. We met through mutual friends thirty some years ago, and became instant pals.

Her friendship has never wavered. She's been my caregiver when I was single, has encouraged me in whatever it was I wanted to do, and stuck by me when times in my life were the toughest.

Gleny, my dearest friend, you are the best. I am blessed.

ACKNOWLEDGMENTS

Thanks to Lorraine Harris, Julie McGlone, Christie Seiler-Boeke, Peggy Hatfield, Angela Hauzer, and Nancy Snyder, members of my writing group, The Write Corner. Without your encouragement, critique, love and support, none of my books would have made it to the publisher. You ladies are the best! These women are all published authors with books for purchase on Amazon, Kindle and Nook.

Many thanks to Maryann Marsh and Marty Orr of TMMA Farms in Oxford, FL. Maryann is a wealth of information on Alpacas. She is always gracious and kind to me, even when I feel like I'm being a pest. Marty is kind and a good-looking cowboy.

If you're ever in the area and love Alpacas, please visit their farm. You'll be glad you did. Their website: www.tmmafarms.com.

Thank you to Retired USMC Gunnery Sergeant, Richard Greenberg, for helping me with issues on PTSD and other related Marine Corps authenticity. Rick is a published author. His website is www.rickgreenbergauthor.com.

Thank you to my editor, Marie Tennant. She has the most difficult job of all. Making sense of my book and wielding her red pen.

Last but not least, my family who encourages me to follow my dreams, whatever they may be. I love you all.

OTHER WORKS BY SHARON ALLEN

NOVELS:

DETOURS OF THE HEART

STONY CREEK DINER

SHORT STORIES:

FOR THE LOVE OF SCOTT

JOURNEYS – AN ANTHOLOGY OF SHORT STORIES

A BOOK WRITTEN BY THE VILLAGE WRITERS

CHAPTER 1

SAWYER MACKENZIE LEANED FORWARD and reached for the barf bag nestled among the Skyline Shopping Mall and Welcome Aboard magazines. *One more downdraft, and I'm gonna' lose it*, she thought, grabbing the bag and placing it in front of her mouth.

White-knuckled, she clung to the armrest as the plane bucked and bounced through the turbulence, making its way through the mountain gaps down into Bozeman, Montana. Several of the passengers shouted "whoa" as the prop flight hit the downdrafts.

Taking a quick glance out the tiny window, Sawyer saw white, puffy clouds and occasional peaks of massive rock formations below her. She had a sinking feeling that at any minute the plane would scrape the tip of one of the mountains sending them hurtling into the ground at breakneck speed.

The thought flooded her with sheer terror. Beads of perspiration broke out on her forehead and nose, and her bowels shuddered. Silently she prayed. *Please God, do not let me mess my pants! Get this plane on the ground, and let me out of here.*

IT HAD BEEN A long day, especially for someone petrified of flying. She'd left her apartment in Florida at 6 a.m. and boarded her flight at Orlando International Airport at eight. The hour and a half trip to Atlanta had been uneventful, so her frayed nerves had begun to calm by the time they landed.

They arrived at terminal A and her connecting flight departed from terminal D. Hurrying through the Jetway, she shifted her backpack and sprinted through the airport, stopping for a moment to suck in a deep breath of air.

Reaching her destination, she flopped down on an empty chair and looked around for her gate number. Panic struck her. *Where's the gate?* She glanced at her boarding pass. *It's says right here, Terminal D, Gate 11. There is no Gate 11!*

She spied the only person in the terminal who might be able to help her. Sawyer rushed over to a young woman dressed in a blue Delta uniform. "Could you please tell me where Gate 11 is?"

The woman pointed to the left. "This is Gate 15, and 11 is four gates down that way."

"Thanks." Hurriedly approaching her gate, she heard a voice announcing that Flight 1127 was about to board.

SAWYER HEARD A WHINE and then a loud thud. *What in hell was that?* She gripped the armrest tighter with one hand, the other hand holding the bag over her mouth. *I am never flying again. Never, never, never! I'll drive to the ends of the earth first.*

"It's okay, dear. The noise you heard was the landing gear engaging," her elderly female seatmate told her. She patted Sawyer's hand. "We're almost there. In just a couple of minutes we'll be on the ground."

That's what I'm afraid of, she thought.

"Welcome to beautiful Bozeman," announced the captain over the loudspeaker. "The sun is shining with temperatures in the high 50s. It's a great day for fishing, hiking, or spending time with loved ones. Thank you for flying Delta Airlines. We love to fly and it shows. Enjoy your stay and we hope to see you again."

It'll be a cold day, Sawyer told herself. *I'll hitchhike first.*

The plane set down with a subtle bump and rolled down the runway until it came to a stop. The pilot turned the plane and taxied to the terminal.

"Please keep your seat belts fastened and stay seated until the plane comes to a complete stop," the flight attendant instructed.

Sawyer was one of the last people to get off the plane. She walked down the steps to the baggage area where she was supposed to meet Sheriff George Logan from Stony Creek. Looking around she spotted him, dressed in his uniform, holding a large sign that read, Sawyer Mackenzie. Welcome to Montana.

She smiled and walked over to him. "Hello there." She stuck out her hand. "I'm so glad to finally be here. It was a long flight."

George Logan frowned, clearly puzzled why this pretty, young woman wanted to shake his hand, telling him she was glad to be here. He glanced around, certain she had mistaken him for someone else. However, he couldn't help himself as he gave her the once-over. He was, after all, only fifty-four years old and he wasn't dead yet. She was about five-five, not an ounce of fat on her, had sparkling blue eyes, red hair and a sprinkling of freckles across the bridge of her tiny nose. Oh yeah, and that slow, sexy smile of hers made him feel like a teenager all over again.

Clearing his thoughts, George said, "I'm sorry, Ma'am, were you speaking to me?"

"Are you Sheriff Logan?"

"I am."

"Well, hello again, I'm Sawyer Mackenzie from Florida. I'm pleased to meet you."

George was glad he didn't blurt out what he was thinking. *"But you're a GIRL! How the hell did I miss that when I hired this new deputy sight unseen?"*

One of his deputies had resigned and he needed a replacement right away. The sheriff did something he had never done before. He had placed an ad on the internet hoping for a quick response. Deputy Sawyer Mackenzie from Florida answered, had good credentials, and from the name, George assumed he was hiring a male. He sure got that one wrong. Now what was he going to do?

In the few minutes it took George to respond, he hoped his expression and tone didn't convey what he was thinking. *Why did parents use boy names for their baby girls and why did women have to work in jobs that used to be traditionally male?* In today's climate of women's equality, he knew better than to utter his chauvinistic attitude.

After getting over the shock of Sawyer Mackenzie being a female, George shook the woman's extended hand. Trying to cover up his surprise, he said, "Of course you're Sawyer Mackenzie. Pleased to meet you, too. Welcome to Montana."

CHAPTER 2

SADIE ABBOTT PARKER BUSIED herself in the spare room of her large two-story farmhouse. She and her husband, Charlie, had offered to rent a room to the newly hired deputy who would be arriving that day. She hummed while dusting the antique furniture, putting hangers in the closet, and making up the bed with fresh sheets from the clothesline. She held the linens up to her nose and inhaled. “Mmmm, these smell so good.”

Sadie continued about the room, adding a clock to the bedside stand and a few *Field and Stream* magazines for her renter to browse through at his leisure. She couldn’t remember a time when she’d been so happy. She smiled, thinking about her new husband.

Several years ago, she and Charlie had lost their spouses. Sixty-nine-year-old Sadie was content running the General Store she had owned with her deceased husband, Cutter Abbott. She had no plans of remarrying. Sadie was financially secure, and more so when she turned her antiquing hobby into a profitable venture. She added a vintage shop to the general store and filled it with toys, games, and other sundries from the past. The locals and out-of-towners loved browsing through the store, reminiscing about times forgotten.

Things changed when Charlie Parker, ten years her senior, started coming by the store. To her surprise, he awoke feelings she thought were dead, and it was the same for him. It took him a while before he asked her on a date, and two years later, he asked her to marry him. They surprised the whole town when they married at the annual Christmas Ball.

"Sadie, Sadie. You home?" her husband of five months hollered up to her, interrupting her happy thoughts.

"I'm up here, Charlie, spiffing up the spare room for the new deputy. He and George should be here anytime now." She gave the room a quick once-over and closed the door.

"Come on down and have a cup of coffee with me, darlin'. That new deputy isn't gonna' care how the room looks as long as he has a bed to lie in and a place to hang his hat. I don't want you getting yourself all worn out."

WHILE CHARLIE WAITED FOR her to join him in the kitchen, he poured them a cup of coffee. He put a few chocolate chip cookies on a plate and seated himself at the table. He took a long sip of the steaming black liquid. "Dang…Dang it all," he sputtered, pushing away from the table and fanning his tongue and lips with his hand.

Sadie stood in the doorway, grinning at her husband. He had been such a sweetheart, agreeing to move into her farmhouse instead of living at his ranch after they were married. According to him, he did it because it was closer to the General Store, but she suspected he did it because he knew she wasn't ready to move.

With a half-smirk on her face she said, "Hot enough for ya?"

He spun around. Peering over his glasses, his bushy white brows drew together in a scowl. "Are you making fun of me?" He fanned his mouth again.

Sadie burst into laughter. "Charlie, you do make me wonder how you ever got along without me." She crossed the kitchen, put her arms around her husband and gave him a passionate kiss, making the old man's knees wobble.

Holding her close, he nuzzled her neck and whispered into her ear.

Sadie turned red and cuffed him on the arm. "Get away with you," she laughed, lightly pushing him toward the table. She sat down, picked up her coffee and blew gently into the hot liquid. "This is how you do it so you won't burn your tongue." She grinned at him over her cup.

"You are a wicked woman. Do you know that?" Charlie pretended to be angry, but Sadie knew better.

Just then, they heard the old hand-turn doorbell.

"That must be Sheriff Logan and the newcomer. George had to drive to Bozeman to pick him up," Sadie told Charlie.

"Well, let's go greet them."

She removed her apron, hung it on a hook in the kitchen and followed her husband into the living room. He opened the door and standing on the porch was George and an extremely pretty, young woman.

George cleared his throat before speaking. "Sadie, Charlie, let me introduce you to Sawyer Mackenzie, our new deputy."

"Well, I'll be danged," Charlie muttered, grinning from ear to ear and slapping his leg with his hand.

Sadie elbowed him in the ribs. Charlie grabbed his side and grimaced in pain. Extending her hand, she smiled and greeted the deputy warmly, "Welcome to Stony Creek, Miss Mackenzie. It's so nice to finally meet you."

"I guess I'm not who any of you expected, but thank you for the nice welcome."

Sadie put her arm around the deputy's shoulder. "Come on in, dear," she told her, ushering Sawyer past the men, right through the living room and into the warm kitchen. "Have a seat. Would you like coffee or tea, something cold to drink?"

"Coffee would be great, thanks. It's been a long day. I could use a little pick me up."

Sadie grabbed a mug from the cupboard and filled it. Passing the cup to Sawyer she said, "Be careful it's hot. You don't want to burn your tongue."

Charlie, on his way into the kitchen, let out a strangled cough and Sadie laughed.

Sawyer looked at them.

"Private joke, honey," Sadie told her.

"This smells delicious," Sawyer said, blowing cautiously on the steaming coffee.

Sadie glanced over at Charlie and raised her eyebrows as if to say, "See."

George came into the kitchen after depositing Sawyer's bags in the living room. "Miss Mackenzie, I'll give you a couple of days to rest, but on Monday I expect to see you at my office and ready to go to work."

"Sheriff Logan, first of all, we need to dispense with the formalities. Please call me Sawyer. Secondly, I don't need time off. I need to get started as soon as possible, if that's okay with you."

"Fine, ah, Sawyer. Charlie or Sadie will show you the way to the office. You won't be able to miss it. We only have one main street in Stony Creek."

"Good. I'll be there tomorrow. What time?"

"How about eight?"

"Eight it is. I'll see you then."

George said his good-byes to the women and went out the front door. Charlie followed him outside. "As that guy on TV would say, 'What the hell were you thinking?'" he asked.

"I have no idea. I don't see how I could have missed the fact that she is a woman, and a very pretty one at that. With a name like Sawyer, who would expect a filly like her to come bounding off the plane? Abigail is going to kill me when she sees Sawyer Mackenzie."

"I reckon Abigail will know all about Miss Mackenzie before you're out of the driveway," Charlie chuckled. "This little piece of news will be buzzing all over town like a bee in a jar. By sundown, everyone will know."

"I'm afraid you're right. I'd better stop at the General Store and buy some flowers for my wife before I throw my hat in the door."

"That's probably a good idea," Charlie acknowledged. "I'd better get inside and take the luggage upstairs before I'm in trouble. Good luck to you, Georgie." Charlie let out a boisterous laugh before letting himself into the house.

CHAPTER 3

"I SUPPOSE YOU'RE SHOCKED that I'm a woman," Sawyer commented to Sadie who took a thoughtful sip of her coffee. "The Sheriff sure was," she grinned.

"Well, to be honest, I am. Sure wish I could have been there to see the look on George's face when you got off that plane." She chuckled. "It must have been a hoot."

"It was kind of funny," Sawyer laughed. "He looked like he wanted to run when I introduced myself, but he managed to stay composed like I was just who he expected."

"I'm sure you're qualified for the job or you wouldn't have been hired. We need a new deputy. Tucker Murphy quit. He was a nice young man and all, but after he witnessed the motorcycle death of a local man, he never got over it. Tucker was riddled with guilt, felt like he should have been able to do more." She shook her head. "There was nothing he could have done. The minute Taylor Boone hit that tree he was a goner."

Sadie's Border collie, Sassy, walked into the kitchen and sniffed at Sawyer. Deciding she was a friend, Sassy lay on the floor next to her.

Sawyer reached down and stroked the dog's head. "Witnessing your first fatality is tough. It sticks with you for a while, but you do get over it. That's why I left Florida. The drive-by shootings, senseless murders, and home invasion robberies are daily occurrences down there. I found myself becoming immune to it all and I didn't want to feel that way. You know, just another day at the office."

She paused and took another sip of her coffee. "Two months ago, my friend and colleague was murdered after a routine traffic stop. That's when I knew I had to leave. I didn't take this job in Stony Creek just because I wanted a change of location. I felt it was time to reboot, start my life anew, so here I am." She smiled at Sadie.

"I don't think you'll have to deal with all that in our little town or the surrounding areas," Sadie told her. "Of course, every now and then bad things do happen, but not every day. Oh goodness, my manners are terrible," she said to Sawyer, shaking her head and pushing away from the table. "Are you hungry?"

"I could use a bite to eat, if it wouldn't be any trouble."

"Our granddaughter, Meredith, owns a diner outside of town. The food is wonderful and it will give you a chance to meet a few of the townspeople. Unless you're too tired, that is. I can rustle us up something to eat in a jiffy if you'd rather stay in."

"I'd love to go to the diner, but I would like to freshen up a little before we leave, if that's okay."

"Of course, let's go upstairs to your room," she pointed the way. "I'll show you where everything is that you'll need."

After leaving Sawyer in her room, Sadie went back downstairs to find Charlie. He was asleep in his chair, Sassy curled up on his feet. Sadie frowned. She was worried about her husband. He didn't seem to have much energy lately and fell asleep at the drop of a hat. Somehow, she was going to get him to see Doc Webster. If he wouldn't go to the office, then she'd ask the doc to come to the house. Charlie could be a stubborn old goat when he wanted to be, but she could be just as stubborn.

"Charlie." She gently shook him awake.

"Huh? What's the matter?"

"Nothing, honey. We're going to take the new deputy to the diner for supper. She's freshening up and I want you to do the same."

"Okay, I'm awake," he said, lifting himself out of the overstuffed chair.

Sadie thought his words sounded a little slurred. "Are you okay? You feel all right?" She felt his brow to see if he was running a fever. He wasn't.

"Quit fussing over me, woman," he answered her gruffly, pulling away from her touch. "If I don't feel good, you'll be the first to know. How's that?"

"That's fine, you old buzzard," she answered curtly, stomping her feet on the way to the kitchen, feelings a bit hurt at the way he spoke to her. Since it was so unnatural for him to behave that way, she knew something was going on. She would contact Doc Webster first thing in the morning.

GEORGE LOGAN TURNED OFF the patrol car in front of his house on Cripple Creek Road. He leaned across the seat and pulled a comb from the glove box. He glanced in the rear view mirror and gave his hair the once-over. *Looks like a little thinning going on up there,* he thought, patting the top of his head, *but when you got it, you got it.* He grinned at himself.

Grabbing the bouquet of flowers off the passenger seat, he opened the car door and exited. Walking up the path to his house, he noticed Abigail standing behind the screen door watching him.

"Hey, Abs, how's your day been going?"

She opened the door for him and he leaned in to kiss her cheek.

"Gotcha' something," he said, pushing the flowers into her hands. "Aren't you going to say anything?" George was nervous as a turkey at Thanksgiving time.

"They're lovely, George. My day has been fine.

Yours?" Her blue eyes sparkled as she spoke to him, but he was too nervous to notice she was teasing him.

"Ah, well, to say that this day has been a regular one, would be telling a lie." He paced back and forth and finally blurted out, "The new deputy is a GIRL!"

Abigail had received more than one phone call with the news, but she was having a good time watching her husband squirm before letting him off the hook. "A girl, huh? Is she pretty?"

George chewed on his lower lip and his eyes held hers for a moment before he turned away. "Yup."

"What's that? Did you say she's not only a woman, but that she's pretty, too?"

George was getting tired of the interrogation. He turned to look at his wife. "She's got damned good qualifications and I'm going to give her a chance. You got a problem with that?"

Abigail's face broke into a huge smile. "None whatsoever, sweetheart. I'm sure if you had realized she was a female, she'd *still* be in Florida. It'll be interesting to see how well she works out. We need some new blood in this town."

"Well, I'm glad that's out in the open. You gonna' feed me before I head back to the office?"

"I have a stew simmering on the stove right now. Oh, and I love my flowers. Thanks." She walked over to George, placed her hands on his face and drew his mouth down to meet hers.

CHARLIE, SADIE AND SAWYER huddled together in the front seat of Nellie Belle, Charlie's 1938 red Ford truck. Since his marriage to Sadie, and to keep her quiet, he'd replaced the broken down old seat with the springs sticking through it. There wasn't much left of Nellie, but she'd been faithful for many years, and he wasn't about to quit on her because he had a new wife.

"How far is it to the diner?" Sawyer asked.

"About a mile out of town," Sadie answered. "We'll take you down Main Street on the way so you can have a look around. Stony Creek is a wonderful little town full of friendly people. I know you'll like it here."

"Ever been to a diner?" Charlie asked her.

"Can't say that I have, but I'm looking forward to it."

Rounding a bend, they drove into Stony Creek and started down the main street. "Over there on the left is the General Store and Vintage Shop. I own both of them," Sadie told her. "I hope you'll stop in and have a look around when you get a minute. There's the drugstore, next to it the Powder Horn Café and across the street is the Smokin' Barrel Saloon," she said, pointing in their direction. "We have five churches, two banks, a few specialty shops, clothing store, and an elementary and a high school."

Sawyer sat quietly, her mouth agape at the small picturesque cowboy town before her. She'd seen towns like this in old Western movies, but surely didn't think one still existed. Wooden sidewalks and hitching posts stood outside of each business, some with a horse attached to them. "This town is amazing," she told them. "Where's the sheriff's office?"

"We'll be going by it in a minute. It's at the end of the street," Sadie told her.

I'm going to love it here. It might be a culture shock in the beginning, but I have a feeling I'm going to live here the rest of my life.

"There's where you'll be working," Charlie told her, pointing out the sheriff's office.

Sawyer glanced at the building with its Montana Sheriff's Dept. emblem emblazoned on a big picture window. George was standing by the window and waved to them as they drove by.

"Think you made a good decision?" Sadie asked.

"I know I did. It'll be good to start working again."

"Here we are, Stony Creek Diner coming up." They pulled into a large parking lot and Charlie turned off the ignition.

"Wow, look at this place," Sawyer exclaimed. "I've never seen anything like it."

"Meredith's mother, my daughter, Velvet, bought it for her before she died," Charlie told her. "Meredith had come home from Florida for the funeral, expecting to stay only a month, and it's been almost a year now."

"Where in Florida?"

"Key West," Sadie piped in. "She was a chef at the Grappling Hook. Ever heard of it?"

"Sorry, no. I've never been to Key West, but it was on my bucket list until I moved out here."

"Well, let's go in and get some grub." Charlie rubbed his belly. "I'm hungry as a bear."

The three of them made their way up the small incline to the diner's entrance. Charlie held the door open for the women; Sadie went in first, Sawyer following behind her. The diner was at near capacity since it was suppertime.

Charlie and Sadie waited until their granddaughter approached them. Sadie had called her earlier letting her know about the new deputy. Smiling, Meredith grabbed Sawyer's hand and held it warmly. "Hi, I'm Meredith Banning. You must be Sawyer Mackenzie. Welcome to Montana and Stony Creek Diner."

"Hey, everyone, meet our new deputy, Sawyer Mackenzie," Meredith addressed her patrons.

You could have heard a pin drop. Everybody stopped eating and simply stared, mouths open. Meredith put her hands on her hips and admonished her friends. "Is this any way for you to welcome her, silence and gawking?"

Looking a bit sheepish, they gave her a wave, said "hey" or "welcome," before going back to their meals.

Meredith noticed a couple of the men continued to

stare at Sawyer, especially Doc Webster. She smiled, thinking his eyeballs were about to pop out of his head. She'd bet his blood pressure had gone up a notch or two if the flush on his face was any indication. She had a feeling Doc would find a way to introduce himself to Sawyer the first chance he got.

CHAPTER 4

MEREDITH LED THEM TO an empty booth in the back of the diner. They slid onto the red leather seats, Charlie and Sadie on one side and Sawyer, sitting on the opposite side, faced the door.

A pretty, blond waitress hurried over with menus and glasses of water. "Howdy, folks. So glad to see you." After setting the tumblers down, she smiled at Sawyer, and stuck out her hand. "Pleased to meet you, Deputy. I'm Carrie Boone."

"Hi, Carrie," Sawyer responded extending her hand. "Happy to meet you."

"Tonight's special is pan-fried brown trout, mashed potatoes, and green beans. Can I start you off with something to drink?"

"Coffee for me," Sawyer told her.

"Make that all the way around," Charlie said.

"Okay, three coffees coming up."

"I love this place," Sawyer said, glancing around the diner.

The stainless steel walls sparkled, and a long, stone counter with red leather stools took up one side of the room. The front of the counter was red and white ceramic tiles as was the floor below it, laid out in an intricate pattern. Across the room were red and white tables and chairs and a few red leather booths with a personal jukebox on the wall in each seating area. For twenty-five cents, patrons could have their choice of three songs. The jukeboxes were a big hit with the customers and music was always playing.

"Did you say Meredith's mother gifted this diner to her?" Sawyer questioned. "I wonder where she found it. It's a great place and certainly a conversation piece."

Charlie glanced over at Sadie. "Maybe we should let Meredith tell you about the diner, when you get to know her better."

"Oh sure, okay. I didn't mean to be nosy. It's just that this is such a unique eatery and in the middle of Montana, too."

Carrie returned with the coffee and took their orders. "Won't be but a few minutes," she told them heading toward the kitchen.

"The diner isn't always open at this hour," Sadie told Sawyer. "Meredith usually closes around two in the afternoon so the Powder Horn Café can get the dinner crowd. It works well for everyone. She decided to stay open tonight since you were coming to town."

"That's so nice of her." Sawyer yawned and covered her mouth. "I'm sorry," she apologized. "It's been a long day and the two-hour time difference isn't helping. That's something I'll need to get used to."

The door opened and Sawyer looked up. Her heart skipped a beat when a gorgeous cowboy walked into the diner and took a seat at the counter. "Who is *that*?" she asked Sadie. "He's handsome." She could feel saliva filling her mouth. She hoped she wouldn't drool and make a fool of herself.

Sadie looked up. "Oh, that's Jethro Byrd, a local rancher and former marine. He's a nice person, but a confirmed bachelor. He also has a bit of an attitude, downright surly at times. You should probably steer clear of him."

"Hmmm," Sawyer mused, intrigued. He had the bluest eyes she'd ever seen; ice blue eyes, which she bet would look right through you. He had salt and pepper hair, parted in the middle and cut short on the sides and in the back. He appeared to be around six feet, and well built in all the right places. Nice butt, too. Sawyer couldn't take her eyes off him.

Doc Webster, who couldn't take his eyes off the deputy, noticed her interest in Jethro. This might be a bit of a challenge, he considered.

Carrie interrupted Sawyer's lustful thoughts when she set their orders in front of them. "Can I get you anything else?"

"I'll have a little more coffee, please," Sawyer answered

When Carrie grabbed the coffee pot from the burner, she leaned against the counter and glanced at Jethro. "Did you see the new deputy Sheriff Logan hired?" she whispered, jerking her head to the right. "She's real pretty."

Carrie believed Jethro needed a woman to soften him up. She'd thought about him for herself at one time, but then she fell in love with the Reverend Anderson.

He turned and looked at the deputy.

Sawyer had just bitten into her burger, and nearly choked, when she noticed the cowboy watching her with a raised eyebrow and a scowl on his face.

What an arrogant jerk, she thought. Sawyer glared right back, even though she was feeling all shaky inside.

Jethro's lip curled in amusement and when Carrie returned to the counter, he frowned at her question.

"See, I told you she was pretty. What do you think?" Carrie asked with a slight smile on her face.

"What? Are you kidding me? George must be out of his mind hiring a female for the job," Jethro snorted.

"Well, she's here to stay. That's what I hear anyway." Carrie noticed Jethro hadn't answered her question.

"Humph! Would it be okay if I ordered now?" he asked sarcastically.

"Sure, whenever you're ready." Carrie grinned as she wrote down his order of pan-fried trout.

"What the heck are you grinning about?"

"Nothing," she replied innocently. "This will be ready in two shakes," she said, walking to the order window. "Order up! We have a grumpy old buck out here who's hungry," she called to Sandra Weaver who was cooking.

Charlie, Sadie, and Sawyer finished their meal and prepared to leave. As they made their way to the door, Meredith stopped them. "Once you're settled in," she said to Sawyer, "please come by my house for a visit. Gramps or Sadie will show you where I live. I'd love to show you around."

"Thanks, that sounds great," she agreed. "Give me a week or so to get acclimated and I'll give you call. How's that sound?"

"Wonderful. I'll look forward to hearing from you. By the way, have you met Jethro Byrd?" He was sitting at the end of the counter and couldn't ignore the introduction. Meredith patted him on the shoulder, forcing him to turn around. "Jethro, this is Sawyer Mackenzie, our new deputy. She's staying with Gramps and Sadie until she finds a place of her own."

He nodded. "Howdy." His face was as cheerful as an open grave.

"He speaks," Sawyer said, amused at his discomfort.

Meredith, Gramps, and Sadie exchanged glances.

What was she doing? It wasn't like her to be sarcastic or mean. "Sorry, I didn't mean to be rude," she told him.

"Forget it," he growled. He turned his back to them and resumed eating.

"He sure is a friendly one," Sawyer whispered to Meredith, "a barrel of laughs I'll bet." She could see his jaw muscle flexing so she knew he had heard. Thinking that she'd made one enemy for the day, she turned to Charlie and Sadie, "I'm ready to go now if you are. Meredith, thanks for everything. I'll be calling you."

Glancing over his shoulder, Jethro watched Sawyer walk out the door. For whatever reason, the woman's words had gotten under his skin, putting him in a foul mood. “What an uppity twit,” he grumbled.

CHAPTER 5

THE BEDSIDE ALARM WOKE Sawyer out of a sound sleep. She tapped the snooze button as she snuggled back down into the bed, hoping for ten more minutes. She heard a soft tap on the door. “Yes?”

The door opened a crack. “Time to get up, sleepy head,” Sadie whispered to her. “The coffee is brewing and blueberry muffins are in the oven.”

Sawyer sat up and stretched. “Thanks. I’ll be down in a short while. I’m going to jump in the shower.”

“Okay, dear. Take your time.”

Sawyer glanced at the clock. It read 5:00 a.m. *Ghastly hour to be up*. Sawyer was used to working second shift and usually slept in until at least ten, but she did promise Sheriff Logan she’d be at the office by eight. As the thought crossed her mind, she began to get butterflies in her stomach. Starting work today as the new deputy in Stony Creek, she desperately hoped she’d made the right decision by moving across the country and leaving her old life behind.

“YOU NERVOUS?” SADIE ASKED Sawyer as they were driving to town.

“No, just excited. I haven’t worked in a couple of months and I’m anxious to get busy again.”

"How do your folks feel about you moving this far away?"

"My parents divorced when I was ten. My mother died a few years ago, and my father was never around much. I think he remarried."

"Sorry for opening that can of worms," Sadie apologized. "Sometimes I'm just a nosy old woman."

"That's okay. I don't have any secrets. I'm sure at some point in time as we get to know each other better, I would have told you anyway."

They turned a corner onto Main Street and Sadie pulled up in front of the Sheriff's office. "Here you are," she smiled. "You're going to do just fine, I know it. Give us a holler when you're ready to go home and either Charlie or I will pick you up."

"Thanks. I do have to see about getting a car, and soon. I don't want to be a burden to anyone."

"Oh honey, you're not a burden," Sadie patted Sawyer's arm. "We're delighted you're here and more than happy to help until you get settled. Don't you fret about it one little bit."

"Thanks, Sadie. I'd better get going now. I don't want to be late my first day."

"Have a good one." Sadie waved good-bye.

SAWYER OPENED THE DOOR to the sheriff's office and stuck her head inside. There didn't seem to be anyone around. "Hello?" Hearing no answer, she walked in.

Three desks in the outer office were unoccupied. A big, bulky mahogany desk and black leather chair in the inner office, which she assumed was the sheriff's, were also empty. Sawyer smelled freshly brewed coffee coming from a back room, and walked toward the aroma. She was about to enter when George came out.

"Holy shit! You scared me," he barked, sloshing some of

his coffee onto the floor.

"I'm sorry," she groaned. Spying a roll of paper towels on a table, she grabbed several to wipe up the spill.

"Never mind, I'll take care of it," George said, removing the towels from Sawyer's hand. He threw them on the floor, and with his foot swished them back and forth to wipe up his mess. "There, good as new." He picked up the towels and threw them into a wastebasket. "Do you want a cup of coffee?" He glanced at his watch and looked at his new deputy. "Right on time. I like that."

"Thanks. It's one of my virtues, being on time that is," she assured him. "I think I'll get that coffee now if it's okay."

"Sure, fine. When you're ready, I'll swear you in." He watched Sawyer, dressed in her jeans and long sleeved shirt, as she went to the back room for her coffee. No way did he have a uniform that would fit this tiny woman. He'd have to order one and have it delivered by FEDEX first thing tomorrow morning.

Sawyer went into the back room and picked up one of the many cups lying helter-skelter on a cluttered counter. Looking inside a cup, she made a face and put it down. She grabbed another and it was the same. Days-old coffee stains rimmed the edges of the mugs. One cup looked like it had something growing inside it. She grimaced as she walked to the sink. There was no dish detergent available so she did the best she could, using her hand and hot water to get the cup clean. She made a mental note to bring in some dish soap tomorrow. She poured herself a cup and walked back into the office.

"Sorry about the mess out there. We guys aren't too particular about cleaning up."

"Ya think?" she replied.

George shot her a disapproving look because of her tone. He didn't like sarcasm, especially coming from a woman.

"Sorry," she said quickly, knowing she'd have to curb her city girl attitude if she was going to make it in Montana.

The front door opened and a middle-aged woman entered. "Morning," she said, placing her handbag full of knitting supplies on one of the desks. "You must be the new deputy. I'm Vivian, dispatcher." She grabbed Sawyer's hand and pumped it up and down in a friendly handshake. "It'll be good to have another woman around here. Don't let him scare you off."

George butted in. "I would have introduced you if you'd given me a minute." As much as he didn't like sarcasm, Vivian could get away with anything. They had worked together for twenty years and over time became family, like brother and sister.

"Oh sure. Right, George," Vivian said, winking at Sawyer as she headed toward the kitchen.

Fifty-four-year-old Vivian Brown was single, a tall, big-boned woman with huge breasts and long brown hair that settled just at the top of her wide bottom. Her mannerisms were more masculine than feminine, and at one time, rumor had it that she might be a lesbian. The men must not have thought so because they buzzed around her like bees after nectar, even though her personality tended to be a bit flippant.

Sawyer didn't move, didn't know what to say, so stood silently waiting to see what was going to happen next.

The front door opened and two deputies entered the building. Sawyer surmised they were in their mid to late thirties.

George quickly introduced them. "This here is Ed Lewis and Pete Tucker. They've been with me for nearly ten years."

The men murmured something about welcome to the fold, and shook hands with her. Earlier that morning while having breakfast at the diner, they questioned George's judgment about keeping a female on staff. "I sure don't think it's a good idea," Pete had said. "The minute he found out she was a woman he should have sent her packing. But he's the boss."

Ed had agreed. "Guess we'll have to see how it plays

out."

"READY TO MAKE IT official?" George asked her a little while later.

"I sure am." Sawyer said.

"Ed and Pete will be witnesses. Let's get started then."

"Raise your right hand and repeat after me. I, Sawyer Mackenzie, do solemnly swear that I will support and defend the Constitution of the United States…"

Sawyer repeated the words George instructed her to say.

"and the Constitution of the State of Montana against all enemies, foreign and domestic; that I will bear true faith and allegiance to the same, and that I will obey the orders of the president of the United States and the governor of the State of Montana."

Sawyer inhaled a deep breath before going on. "That I make this obligation freely, without any mental reservation or purpose of evasion; and that I will faithfully discharge the duties of the office of Sheriff in the county of Gallatin upon which I am about to enter, so help me God."

"Welcome, Deputy Mackenzie," George said, smiling at her. The other deputies gave her a light pat on her back before leaving to get back to work.

"See you around," Ed Lewis told her.

"Thanks," she replied.

"Well, unfortunately, I don't have a uniform to fit you so I'm going to order one. You'll need to help me with that, size and all. In the meantime, here's your shield, belt, holster and gun."

Sawyer beamed as she pinned the badge on her shirt.

"By the way, a cruiser comes with the job so you won't have to worry about purchasing a vehicle of your own. You will have to get a Montana driver's license though. We can take a ride into Bozeman today and take care of it."

"That would be great. I'm excited to see the surrounding

area. I was too tired yesterday to notice much of anything on our way back from the airport."

"It won't take you too long to find your way around. I'll be riding with you for a few days and then I'll send you out on your own. Let me give Ed a call. I'll have him come back to the office while we're in Bozeman." George headed toward the back.

The door opened and a tall, blond good-looking man in his thirties walked in. "Hi," his face broke into a welcoming smile as he extended his hand to Sawyer. "I'm the doc around here, Elliott Webster. Just wanted to make your acquaintance and welcome you to Stony Creek. My office and house is right down the end of the street."

"Thanks, Dr. Webster," she replied, noticing his rich, brown eyes and long, thick lashes.

"Call me Elliott. There's not much formality around these parts. Anyway, makes me feel old when people call me Doctor Webster."

Sawyer relaxed and smiled back. "Elliott it is, then. Please call me Sawyer."

George came out of the back room with Ed who had just come in the rear door. "Ready for that ride?" he asked Sawyer.

"I am." She turned her attention back to the doctor. "We're off to Bozeman, but thanks for stopping in. I'm sure I'll be seeing you around."

"I hope so," he said.

CHAPTER 6

"THANKS, DOC. I'LL HAVE him there first thing tomorrow morning." Sadie hung up the phone, knowing without a doubt Charlie was going to have a conniption fit when she told him she had made an appointment for him. Well, he could fall down on the floor and throw a tantrum like a two-year-old, but he was going. She'd make sure of it. In her gut and her heart, she knew something was seriously wrong with her husband.

CHARLIE WALKED INTO THE DINER. He needed to talk to his granddaughter. Since she was rarely home, the diner was the best place to catch up with her. He took a seat in a rear booth and picked up a menu stuffed between the salt and pepper shakers. Sadie hadn't been feeding him anything he liked in the past few weeks, and by golly, he was determined to have a decent breakfast, at least one day a week.

Carrie came over with a pot of coffee. She turned over a mug that was upside down on a placemat and filled it with the freshly brewed java. "Hey, Charlie, haven't seen you around for breakfast in a long time. What can I get you?"

"Wife makes me eat at home now," he growled. "Seems like the only thing she can cook these days is oatmeal. I want two eggs over easy, bacon, fried potatoes, and sourdough toast. Make it white," he grumbled in defiance. "Is Meredith out back?"

"She sure is. Want me to tell her you're here?"

"Please."

Charlie picked up a newspaper someone had left on the seat and sipped his coffee, remembering to blow into it. Good coffee. Not that decaf crap. Flipping to the obituary page, he scanned it quickly to make sure his name wasn't in it. He didn't see any of his friends in there either, so it was a good day. He'd been thinking about death a lot lately and couldn't seem to shake the feeling.

"Gramps! Great to see you." Meredith leaned over and gave her grandfather a hearty kiss on the cheek. "How are you?"

"I'm okay, I guess. Do you have a minute to sit down? I got some things I want to talk over with you."

"Sure." Sliding in the seat across from him she said, "Sounds serious." She frowned reaching for his old gnarled hands and held them in hers, softly rubbing his knuckles. "What's going on, Gramps? You're scaring me."

Charlie cleared his throat. "I want you to know that if anything happens to me, the ranch is yours, lock, stock, and barrel."

"What are you talking about?" Meredith questioned, concern in her voice. "What about Sadie? She's your wife now and whatever you have should go to her."

"Don't you worry about Sadie. Cutter left her quite well off and I've added a hefty insurance policy to that. I saw a lawyer last week and had paperwork drawn up so you'll never have to worry about a thing either. You'll be getting a copy in the mail in a few days. Thought I should let you know beforehand."

"Gramps, are you sick?" Meredith's stomach churned, imagining every possible medical ailment.

"I don't think so. It's just that I'm getting older and feel it's time to make sure all my affairs are in order."

"Have you talked this over with Sadie?"

"I will in time," he answered, taking another sip from his mug, but not meeting her eyes.

Carrie interrupted their conversation. "Here's your breakfast, Charlie," placing the delicious meal in front of him. "Enjoy, and I promise I won't tell Sadie you were here." She flashed him a devilish grin as she walked away.

Charlie's mouth watered at the sight of his breakfast fare. He liberally buttered his toast, and pierced his eggs with his fork, watching the yolk slide onto the plate. He dipped a piece of toast into the yellow substance and put it into his mouth, savoring the taste. Licking his lips, *So much better than oatmeal.*

Meredith remained silent as she watched her grandfather devour his breakfast. He acted as if it was his last meal before being dragged off to the gas chamber. Something was definitely wrong, and she wondered if she should call Sadie.

Carrie came over to refill their cups, but they both declined. When she removed Charlie's empty plate from the table, she grinned watching him rub his belly, a look of sheer satisfaction on his face "Glad you enjoyed your meal," she smiled.

"I sure did. Well, guess I'd better be going. Thanks for the talk and the breakfast," he said to his granddaughter. Charlie wiped his mouth with his napkin, left four dollars on the table for Carrie, and scooted out of the booth.

Meredith slid out at the same time.

"Oh, by the way, you and Dakota come by for dinner some evening. He hasn't met the new deputy yet. She's a feisty one," he said smiling.

"Maybe I don't want him meeting her," Meredith laughed. "She's very pretty. I noticed several of the men giving her the eye the night she was in here."

"She started work yesterday. Said she had a great day."

"You sure you're okay, Gramps?" Meredith was still worried and didn't quite believe his story about just getting older. There had to be more to it than that.

"Darlin', if there's anything to worry about, believe me, my wife will let you know. Until you hear from her, don't fret. Think about coming for dinner, and soon."

"I will. Have a great day, Gramps. Weather looks perfect."

Charlie plunked his Stetson on his head, and as he was about to leave, the door opened.

Dakota Morgan clapped Charlie on the back as he came in. "Hey, Gramps, how you doing today?" He looked over at the counter and saw Meredith standing there. He smiled and winked.

"Doing fine, Dakota," Gramps responded. "On my way out to the ranch."

"Say 'hi' to my parents for me, will you? I haven't seen them lately. My fault."

"Sure will. I'll be going now."

DAKOTA LEANED OVER THE COUNTER and planted a light kiss on Meredith's lips.

"Okay you two lovebirds," one of the locals said. "Enough of that stuff. I'm trying to eat my breakfast."

Meredith and Dakota grinned at each other. "Coffee?" she asked, holding out a mug.

"I'd love some. How's your day going?"

"Let's grab a booth," she said softly. She poured them each a cup and walked toward the rear of the diner.

Dakota, confused by her actions, didn't press her until they sat down. "So what's wrong?"

"I'm not sure, but Gramps told me he had been to a lawyer and left the ranch to me. I wonder if he's sick or if something's wrong with his marriage. I hardly believe that's the case, but he sure is acting mysteriously."

"Now don't let your mind play tricks on you or imagine all the worst case scenarios. You have a habit of doing that, you know."

Meredith gave him a dirty look and ignored his comment. "I asked him if Sadie knew all this. He said no, he'd tell her in time."

"Well, then I guess we'll have to wait until one of them tells us what the story is." Dakota, always the logical one, drove Meredith crazy at times. She loved him with all her heart, but every now and then it would be nice if he'd let his imagination run wild like hers did.

"Fine," she muttered. "I'll do all the worrying for the both of us. Wouldn't want *you* to get stressed out, would we?"

Dakota laughed aloud. "What are you getting all stiffed up about? I was only making a point. I don't want you to worry because it's out of your control. We have to be patient and wait."

"I know," she whined. "I have such a difficult time doing that, but you're right."

Dakota slapped a hand to his heart. "Did you hear what you just said?" He laughed again. "I'm right?"

"I think you better drink your coffee and get back to work, if you know what's good for you," she threatened.

"I think you have a point." He finished his coffee and they stood simultaneously. He grabbed her hand and pulled her into the kitchen. Wrapping his arms around her body and holding her closely, he nuzzled her neck until she squealed; then he lowered his mouth to hers in a passionate kiss. When she started to kiss him back, he released her.

"Have a good day, sweetheart," he laughed, blowing her a kiss as he walked out of the kitchen.

"I could kill him when he does that," Meredith said, knees all wobbly.

"If you don't want him," Sandra Weaver, the cook, spoke up, "there are plenty of women out there who would gladly take your place."

"Oh gosh, I forgot you were here," she laughed.

"Guess I was wrapped up in the moment."

CHARLIE PULLED INTO THE driveway after a long day at the ranch, hoping that Sadie had made him a decent meal. He was sweaty and a bit light-headed. He needed some food right now. He leaned over and opened the glove box pulling out a half-eaten Hershey bar and shoving it in his mouth. He laid his head back on the seat. Within minutes, he was feeling much better. There. All I needed was a bit of food. When he looked up, Sadie was on the porch, hands on her hips, waiting. *Oh boy, here we go*, he thought, getting out of the truck.

"Charlie Parker, are you going to tell me what's wrong with you?"

"Been talking to Meredith?" he growled.

"I haven't been talking to anyone except Doc Webster. By the way, you have an appointment with him nine o'clock tomorrow morning. We *are* going to get to the bottom of this. You haven't been yourself in weeks and frankly, you're scaring me to death."

"I will not see Doc tomorrow. You had no right to call him without my permission."

"Your *permission*?" she spat. "I don't need your permission, Charlie Parker, for anything and don't you ever forget it!" She turned on her heel, stomped into the house, and slammed the door in his face.

He trudged up the steps and opened the door. He could hear Sadie crying softly in the kitchen. When he walked in, she lifted the bottom of her apron and quickly wiped her tears. Charlie felt like a total jerk.

"Sadie, I'm sorry. I don't know what's wrong with me lately. Seems like all I do is get mad at you for no reason."

"Are you sorry you married me?" she asked, sniffing and wiping at her nose.

"Oh darlin', no, never. I've loved you for a long time and this past year has been one of the happiest of my life. Don't ever think that."

"I know you don't feel well, Charlie. That's why I made the appointment for you. Please say you'll see him. If not for you, then at least for me?" she pleaded.

Charlie stood in the middle of the kitchen floor, twisting his Stetson round and round in his hands. He looked up at his wife and it broke his heart to see the pain he was causing her. "I'll go, but will you go with me?"

Sadie nodded as the tears streamed down her face again. She held out her arms to her husband and he hurried into them. "Let's not fight again," she said, hugging him tightly. "I'm exhausted."

"I'm hungry." He gave her a quick tap on the butt. "Get me some grub woman."

"Yes, Master," she laughed.

CHAPTER 7

GEORGE SETTLED INTO THE passenger seat and handed the keys to Sawyer. “Here you go. Let’s see what you can do.” He wanted to observe how well she could drive before putting one of his new patrol cars in her possession. It might seem chauvinistic, but he didn’t care. He needed to make sure she could handle the mountainous terrain since part of her responsibilities would involve driving long distances a day.

They drove in comfortable silence along the winding roads leading to Bozeman. George observed Sawyer and she was handling the curves well enough, but the drive through Wilson’s Canyon would test her skills.

“The mountains are so majestic. They remind me of a skyline on a postcard. This country is absolutely beautiful, Sheriff,” she said, breaking the silence as she glanced at the scenery around her. “The old homesteads scattered in the fields, abandoned so many years ago, makes me wonder who lived there and what their lives were like.”

George smiled hearing her gush about Montana, something most of the people living here take for granted. Seeing Montana through her eyes made him proud to be a Montanan.

“Oh, my gosh, look over there. I know they aren’t deer.” She pointed to several tan and white animals running along the hillsides. “Are they antelope?” she asked excitedly. She pulled over to the side of the road to get a better look.

"They sure are," George told her.

"Wow! I've seen them on TV, but never like this. Sure wish I'd brought my camera."

Sawyer admired the animals with their forked horns, and russet-colored bodies with patches of white on them. She noted the white rings around their necks and large white patches on their rumps. The antelopes stopped running and seemed to be checking her out as well.

"Best we get going," George told her.

Sawyer pulled the car back onto the road. Several minutes later, they were in Wilson's Canyon. Over on her right the Jefferson River ran alongside a field. It reminded her of a movie she had once seen, *A River Runs Through It.* She spied a couple of men fly-fishing, the water halfway up their waders.

"George, I have to come back here when I have more time. I'm just blown away by nature in its unspoiled beauty."

At first, it was refreshing watching Sawyer in awe of the scenery, but now he was growing tired of her oohs and ahs and wanted something to eat. "Once you get your bearings, you can drive anywhere you please and take pictures to your heart's content."

Continuing on the tight winding road, Sawyer noticed what appeared to be a large cave in the canyon wall. Some ignorant person had spray painted graffiti on the side of the rock near the opening. Why did people have to destroy what nature had intended?

George could see the wheels spinning in Sawyer's head. "Don't be trying to check this place out," he warned her. "There are snakes in there and God knows what else. Some things are better left alone."

She grinned at George. "Mind reader," she joked.

"Just don't want you getting into trouble," he quipped. "You hungry? I only had coffee this morning, and the old belly is starting to rumble. We could stop at the Three Forks

Café."

"My stomach is making noises, too. Sadie tried to get me to eat before I left, but I didn't want to be late."

"It's just down the road. We'll be there before too long."

As they passed another old homestead, George pointed to it. "That's the old Parker Homestead." Nestled among several cottonwood trees, the main house was a sod-roofed log cabin, and a number of outbuildings dotted the one-acre parcel. "Net and Rosa Parker owned and occupied the property back in the 1900s," he told her.

Sawyer knew she'd be returning to take pictures and walk around the premises. For some reason, these old homes intrigued her. She couldn't wait to venture out on her own. She'd heard there were some ghost towns not too far away. Something else for her to explore.

Thirty minutes later, they pulled into the parking lot of the café. When they entered, several regulars called out to George.

He'd lived in these parts all his life and knew just about everybody. He introduced Sawyer as his newest deputy and several men let out loud wolf whistles. "Don't be getting too frisky with your mouths," he warned them. "Remember, she has a badge, a gun and can arrest the whole lot of you if she has a mind to."

The men laughed, Sawyer blushed, and George directed her to a table. Sawyer glanced at the menu and thought how very different some of the items were, compared to restaurants she'd frequented in Florida. For example, today's special was a Bison burger. Guess it was as good a time as any to try one out.

AFTER THEIR MEAL, THEY headed toward Bozeman again. "We'll take the back way so you can see some of the little towns."

"Show me the way and I'll get us there," Sawyer assured

him.

George went on. "Our department ranges 100+ miles per day in an eight-hour shift, depending on call volume. Right now, there are only four of us, so I'll probably hire more deputies in the future. As our area grows, so will our law enforcement."

Driving further, they came to the little town of Logan. "In its heyday, Logan was a major railroad town. Today it's most popular for its legendary *The Land of Magic Steakhouse*. Best steaks anywhere," George told her. "I bring Abigail there for our anniversary every year. She looks forward to it."

"I'll have to try it," Sawyer replied.

"They hold Annual Branding Parties the first weekend in May and area ranchers leave their marks on the walls of the restaurant. Its lots of fun for some, but a headache for us deputies."

"Why's that?" she asked, as she continued driving.

"Too much celebrating and sometimes things get out of hand. One or two of us are in the area when the partying begins."

"This here is Manhattan," he pointed out, as they continued. "Blink your eyes and that's it."

They rolled through the town of Belgrade and into Bozeman. George directed Sawyer to the County Treasurer's Office where she would obtain her Montana driver's license. The fee was $40.50 for eight years, which Sheriff Logan paid. Sawyer took an eye test, had her picture taken, and turned in her Florida license. In turn, she received her new one. She crinkled up her face at her picture, but beamed when George said, "You're a true Montanan now."

ON THE WAY BACK to Stony Creek Sawyer felt good, as if she had passed a milestone in her life. She was happy and knew in her heart that Montana is where she would grow old.

"George?"

"Yah?"

"Will you put the word out that I'm looking for a house in the Stony Creek area? I'd like something with a little land and a barn. I want a dog and eventually, if I learn to ride, I might buy a horse. I've got some money saved, so I'm ready to look at some places if the price is right."

"Something wrong at Sadie and Charlie's?"

"Oh no, they're wonderful. It's just that I'm used to living alone and miss having my own things.

"You don't ride?" he asked, somewhat incredulous. "Well, we'll have to see about that. You may need to be on horseback one of these days, so the sooner you learn, the better. I'll talk to a couple of folks about giving you lessons."

They pulled up in front of the sheriff's office. "Come on," George said, getting out of the car. "I've got something for you."

She followed him inside and Ed and Pete greeted her. "Did you get your license?" Pete asked.

"Sure did. Piece of cake. I thought I might need to take a road test, but I guess my drive on the way to Bozeman was it, right George?"

"Right," he grumbled from the back room. "Where the hell did I put that package?"

"Need any help?" Ed asked. "He couldn't find his hat if it wasn't on his head," he chuckled.

"I heard that," George yelled.

Sawyer, Ed, and Pete broke into a hearty laughter.

George came out of the back, a FEDEX package in his hands. "Here," he said, thrusting the box at Sawyer. "It's your uniform. I expect you to wear it tomorrow."

"Thanks, George." She smiled, wondering if it was going to fit since he'd obviously taken it upon himself to order without her input.

"You can go home for the day. I'll check around about that thing you were asking me about. By the way," he tossed the car keys to her, "that's your cruiser now." He pointed to the vehicle they had been using all day.

"Thanks. It'll be good having wheels. What time does my shift start tomorrow?"

"Be here at seven. I'll give you a key so you can let yourself in if no one is here."

"Right." Sawyer would be there at six. She intended to clean up the coffee room before she drank another sip out of those hideous stained cups. "Have a good evening and I'll see you in the morning."

DRIVING BACK TO SADIE and Charlie's, Sawyer decided to take a side trip over to the diner. She wanted to meet more of the locals and visit with Meredith.

Walking into the diner, she heard a few soft murmurs, "There's the new deputy" and a couple of "Howdy's." She smiled and nodded, before taking a seat at the counter.

Carrie greeted her. "Coffee?"

"I'd love a cup, thanks. I'd also like one of those muffins, blueberry if you have any."

"We sure do, coming right up."

Sawyer thought Carrie was cute more than pretty with her curly blond hair and petite stature. Carrie brought the coffee and the muffin.

"Can I get you anything else?"

Sawyer shook her head. "Carrie, right?" she asked, taking a sip of coffee.

Carrie smiled. "That's right. You've got a good memory."

"Have you worked here long?"

"Ever since they opened, almost a year ago. I had just lost my husband and was living with my parents. I needed a job so I could get a place for me and my three boys. I think Meredith took pity on me and gave me a chance. My parents were great, but I needed to get out from under them, if you know what I mean."

"I completely understand."

The door to the diner opened and Storm Anderson, the Methodist preacher, came in and took a stool at the counter. Carrie blushed and Storm grinned wider than a Cheshire Cat. "Hey there, Carrie," he said. "How's the day been treating you?"

Sawyer watched the interaction between the two and wondered if something was going on between them. She hadn't missed the blush on Carrie's face.

"Storm, this is Sawyer," she stammered. "Sorry, I forget your last name."

"It's Mackenzie."

"I'll start over," Carrie said apologetically. "Storm, this is Sawyer Mackenzie, our new deputy. Sawyer, this is Reverend Storm Anderson."

Storm put his hand out and Sawyer readily accepted it. "Pleased to meet you, Sawyer. I hope we'll see you at church some Sunday."

Sawyer didn't do church. She'd been raised in a strict religious home with so many don'ts there wasn't room for many dos. When she became an adult, she "backslid," much to her grandparents' chagrin. She never went to church again and doubted she ever would.

"Well, guess it's time for me to get back to Sadie's," Sawyer told Carrie. "Could I have my check, please?"

"We don't charge our law enforcement for coffee or muffins," Carrie told her, "so it's on the house."

"Really? That's very kind. Thank you. By the way, is Meredith in today?"

"Nope. She had errands to run, so she took the day off."

"Please thank her for me and tell her I'll be back in a couple of days to catch up. Nice to meet you, Reverend. Thanks, Carrie."

"Take care," Carrie called out to Sawyer as she was leaving.

Walking to the cruiser, she saw Jethro Byrd step out of

his truck. Sawyer's belly did a little flip-flop. He was a little older than she was, but he was one fine specimen. "Mr. Byrd," she acknowledged with a nod

He never looked her way, but she did hear a muffled "Humph" as he walked past her.

She resisted a strong urge to punch him. What was there about her that made him so angry and why did she care anyway?

"SADIE, YOU HOME?" Sawyer called out when she entered the house.

"Out here in the kitchen, dear."

Sawyer smelled fresh coffee brewing and the aroma from an apple pie wafted through the house as she walked into the kitchen. "Sure smells good in here."

"You're home early," Sadie said.

"George and I went to Bozeman today for my license, so he let me go when we got back."

"What's in the package?"

"My uniform. I was hoping I could try it on and you could tell me how it looks."

"I'd be happy to. Want some coffee first?"

"A little later, if you don't mind. I want to see whether this fits." She hurried upstairs, tore the box open, and held the uniform up in front of her. It looked large to her, but maybe once she had it on it would look better.

A few minutes later, she strode into the kitchen. Sadie took one look at her and burst out laughing. Sawyer stood there with her trousers dragging on the floor, the sleeves of her shirt way below her hands, and the bodice baggy in all the wrong places. "I assume George ordered this?" She couldn't help but grin.

Sawyer, about in tears, nodded. It was just a uniform, but she wanted to look presentable. This made her look not only unprofessional, but she'd be the laughing stock of the town.

God forbid Jethro Byrd should see her in this getup. She pulled at the trousers. "He expects me to wear this to work tomorrow," she sniffled.

"There, there, dear," Sadie patted Sawyer on the back. "I can fix this in no time. A hem here and there, a few tucks, and we'll be in business. Let me get my straight pins and tape measure. Rest assured you'll be able to wear this in the morning if I have anything to say about it."

"Thanks, Sadie. You're a God-send."

CHAPTER 8

"COME ON, CHARLIE," SADIE hollered up to her husband who was taking his sweet time coming downstairs. "We have to be at Doc's at nine." She rinsed her coffee cup, put it in the drainer, let Sassy out, and straightened the morning paper that was scattered on the kitchen table. "Charlie," she called out again.

"Hold your horses, woman," Charlie grumbled. "I heard you the first time. Stomping down the stairs he asked, "You gonna' feed me before we go?"

"No, I'm not. Doc wants you fasting before he draws your blood so he can get an accurate reading. If you eat something, it can throw the numbers off. When we're done, you can go to the diner for breakfast."

"You're not going to eat with me?"

"I have a business to run," she reminded him, "so I'm going to work. I'll grab something later."

"No need for you to be working," he complained, fiddling with the buttons on his shirt.

"You sure are a sour puss this morning. It's been such a joy living with you lately," her voice dripped with sarcasm.

"Well, you're no picnic either, Miss Bossy Boots."

"Look, let's quit arguing and get going. I know this is something you don't want to do, but it's necessary and you're going to do it." Sadie grabbed the truck keys from a bowl on a side table and headed toward the door. "You driving or shall I?" she asked, dangling the keys in front of him like a carrot in front of a mule.

"You wouldn't be able to get out of the driveway in Nellie Belle," he snarled. "She's a one man truck and a loyal one at that. Not like some women I know." He snatched the keys from her hand and stormed out the door.

Finally, they were on their way. Sadie breathed a sigh of relief as she followed her husband down the steps. She prayed Charlie would be okay. She had an idea what might be wrong, but didn't mention it. He never would have believed her anyway, but if Doc verified what she surmised, Charlie would believe him.

THE SIGN ON DOC WEBSTER'S door read *Walk In*. Elliott was waiting for his first appointment, Charlie Parker. Today would be the first time he would see Charlie professionally, even though he'd been practicing here for over three years.

Elliott smiled recalling how his original plan was to stay in Stony Creek for five years, then move on to more lucrative pastures. His plans changed after he began to know his patients and their families who became his friends. Stony Creek was a great place to raise children and he quickly grew to love the tightly knit, small town.

When he hired on as Stony Creek's doctor he had no idea what was in store for him. As one of the only doctors around for miles, he was on call day and night. His duties as a general practitioner required him to use an array of medical skills. His patients depended on him for casting broken bones to delivering babies. On occasion, Elliott would accept payment of produce or other local sundries for his services from those who couldn't ordinarily afford to see a doctor.

On a typical day, he saw fifteen to twenty patients. One morning a week he spent at the local nursing home, checking up on patients and prescribing or renewing medications.

As much as Elliott loved small town living, his wife had hated it. After their first year in Stony Creek, she moved back east and left the boys behind for him to raise. When word got out that the doc in Stony Creek was available, women traveled from miles around to see him about any number of ailments, mostly imagined or made up. He was one of the most eligible bachelors in the county and had amazing brown eyes, or so he'd been told. What woman wouldn't be attracted to him? Elliott was flattered, but sent them on their way.

It had been two years since Lynda left. Elliott had a good life, but in the last few months, he was becoming increasingly lonely. Now that the boys were older, he found he was thinking more about a wife. The new deputy crossed his mind. She was single and not bad on the eyes.

"DOC?" SADIE CALLED OUT. "You here?"

Elliott walked into the waiting room to see Sadie with her hand on Charlie's elbow, ushering him into the office. "Charlie," Elliott offered his hand. "Good to see you. Come on back."

He led them to an examination room. "Why don't you hop up here," Doc said, patting the brown leather table.

Charlie mumbled under his breath but complied.

"So, what seems to be the problem?"

"Ask *her*," he grunted, jerking his chin toward Sadie.

Elliott ignored Charlie's remark and continued to question his patient. He knew he would have to tread lightly with this stubborn old man. "You been feeling okay? Any chest pains or anything different you can think of?"

"Nope."

"*Char-lee*. Tell Doc the truth," his wife urged.

"No chest pains."

"Are you more thirsty than usual?" Doc asked.

"Well, now that you mention it, it does seem like I'm

drinking more water."

"Are you urinating more, too?"

"I guess so. Just told you I was drinking more water," he grunted.

"Have you been more tired than usual?" This exam was like pulling teeth, one at a time.

"Yah, I fall asleep for no reason and can't seem to get out of my own way."

"How long has this been going on?" Doc asked, looking directly at Charlie. Doc felt eye contact was important so his patients would know he was listening, and that he cared about what they were saying. He felt this was especially important to people like Charlie who didn't hold much stock with the medical field to begin with.

"Probably a few months. Sadie wanted me to come in sooner, but I didn't feel it was necessary. If I want to continue living with her, I have no choice, so here I am."

"I have an idea what might be the problem, so I want to do a blood workup on you. Did you eat anything this morning?"

Charlie shook his head.

"Good. I'm going to prick your finger, which will show us your sugar level right now, and then I'll draw your blood and send the other tests to the lab. We'll know the results of those in a few days when you come back for a follow-up."

Charlie raised his eyebrows at the "F" word, follow up, but didn't say anything. He wasn't about to be running to the doctor's office every week.

Elliott cleaned Charlie's middle finger with an alcohol swab and drew a drop of blood with a lancet. He tested it on the glucometer and frowned. Charlie's reading was 502. Much too high.

"Hold still now while we finish up." Doc put a tourniquet around Charlie's arm and placed a soft rubber ball in his hand. "Pump the ball," he told him. Elliott found a good vein. "You can stop pumping now. Here we go, big stick, Charlie," and it was over. He placed a Band-Aid over the puncture, patted the old man on the shoulder, and left the room.

Charlie jumped down from the examining table, unrolled his shirtsleeve, and glanced over at Sadie.

"There, that wasn't so bad was it, sweetie?" she asked.

"I'm hungry," Charlie growled.

Doc entered the room and asked them both to take a seat. "Charlie, I'll get right to it. You have Diabetes Type 2."

"What the hell are you talking about? I don't have diabetes, you moron," Charlie protested, jumping up from his chair and folding his arms across his chest rebelliously.

"He didn't mean that, Doc," Sadie apologized.

"I didn't take it personally, so not a problem. Charlie, you do have diabetes and the sooner we get you started on treatment, the sooner you'll feel better."

Charlie paced around the exam room. An old friend of his had diabetes, lost a foot, then his leg, and eventually died. Losing a limb was not the way Charlie planned to leave this earth, so Doc had to be wrong.

"I'm going to the diner and get something to eat," he said, hand on the doorknob, looking defiantly at his wife and then at the doc.

Sadie bolted across the room and grabbed his arm. "You're doing no such thing, Charlie Parker," she said sternly. "You're going to sit here, listen to Doc, and we're going to take his advice. I know you're scared, but this type of diabetes can be controlled. Now go sit down," she said more softly.

Chastised like a small child, he hung his head and slumped down in a chair. "Sorry, Doc. Had a friend die from diabetes a long time ago. It wasn't pretty."

"I know you're nervous," Elliott said, "and I'm sorry about your friend. However, your numbers are extremely high and we need to get started immediately. I've arranged for your admission to Bozeman Deaconess this afternoon. You need to be there at one o'clock."

Charlie stood. His face went ashen and his hands began to tremble. “I don’t want to go to the hospital, Doc. Can’t we do something here?” he asked, gripping the back of a chair.

Elliott shook his head. “We need to start you on insulin injections to get your numbers under control. Then I hope to put you on oral medication, which should work *if* you stick to a diet and do what I tell you to do. You’ll only have to stay in the hospital a few days.”

“I can’t leave my wife alone,” Charlie protested.

“Charlie Parker,” Sadie chimed in, “I lived alone the past few years until we got married, and, anyway, Sawyer is staying with us so I won’t be alone. I’ll spend as much time at the hospital with you as I can, so don’t be worrying about me.”

“When you get to the hospital, go straight to admissions. I’ll have all the necessary paperwork there. I’ll come in later this evening to check on you.” Doc put his hands on Charlie’s shoulders and looked him in the eyes. “You’re going to be fine,” he promised.

CHAPTER 9

IT WAS STILL DARK out when Sawyer parked the cruiser behind the sheriff's office. When she exited the vehicle, she could hear the high-pitched howling and yelping from a pack of coyotes in the distance. The sound gave her goose bumps and she shivered.

She let herself into the office with the key George provided her the previous day and flipped on the light switch, illuminating the room. Sawyer didn't want to be disturbed at the early hour, so she walked quickly across the room and closed the blinds. If there were an emergency, someone would call or bang on the door.

On a mission to clean up the back room, she reached into her bag and pulled out a bottle of dish detergent and some steel wool. She crossed the room to the sink, filled a plastic basin with hot water, and eased the stained coffee cups down into the soapy liquid. While they soaked, Sawyer filled the coffee carafe with water, poured it into the reservoir, popped a filter in the basket, and measured out four heaping scoops of Columbian coffee. The men would either like how she made it or not, but at least they'd be drinking out of clean cups.

Sawyer admired herself in the full-length mirror in the bathroom. Sadie had performed miracles on her uniform and now it fit perfectly. She would need another uniform soon, but this time *she* would be the one ordering it. She'd learned a lesson having her boss order for her.

It was nearing 7 a.m. and the men would be arriving soon. Opening the blinds, she jumped and let out a loud shriek. Staring in at her, both hands on the window framing his face, was a big, burly man with a bushy grey beard.

"It's okay," he said loudly, holding up both hands and taking a step back. "I didn't mean to scare you. I just wanted to introduce myself."

Sawyer swallowed and unlocked the door, letting the man in.

He offered his hand and gave her a firm, welcoming handshake. "Hi. I'm Samuel Johnson, owner of the Smokin' Barrel Saloon. My wife, Willa Mae, runs the Powder Horn Café across the street from the saloon. Folks around here call me Jigger."

"Pleased to meet you, Mr. Johnson. Nice of you to stop by and say hello." Sawyer tried to maintain a look of calm, but her insides were quaking. Coming from a big city in Florida where killings were a daily occurrence, one couldn't be too careful. She knew things were different here, but it would take some getting used to.

"Please, call me Jigger. Stop by anytime. Willa wants to meet you, too."

"I'll do that. Thank you, ah, Jigger. How did you come by that name?"

"As I just told you, I own the saloon, but I'm also the bartender. I pour whiskey into little shot glasses called jiggers. A long time ago, someone dubbed me with the nickname, Jigger. Can't remember exactly who it was, but the name stuck. I'll be leaving now. Hope to see you soon." He let himself out and Sawyer breathed a sigh of relief. She hadn't realized she'd been so tense.

GEORGE, PETE AND ED arrived at the station shortly after seven. "Any phone calls?" George asked.

"None yet, but I did meet Jigger Johnson. Nice man."

"He sure is. He'd give you the shirt off his back if you needed it. Wait until you meet Willa Mae. You'll like her a lot."

"Jigger said she wants to meet me. I'll introduce myself to her later when I'm walking the beat."

The three men burst into laughter and Pete poked Ed in the ribs. "The Beat! Ha! That's a funny one."

"What's so funny about that?" she snapped, obviously annoyed with their teasing.

"The Beat, as you call it, is Main Street. It might take all of ten minutes to walk from one end to the other."

"Come on, boys," George chimed in. "Give her a break. She's a city girl trying to adapt to our slower way of living. By the way, Sawyer, and please don't arrest me for sexual harassment, but you look good in that uniform. I did one heck of a job picking out the right size." He shot her a triumphant smile.

Sawyer figured George's arm was about to break the way he was patting himself on the back. Deciding she didn't want to burst his bubble, she said nothing. At least not now.

"Good coffee, Sawyer," Ed told her, "although the flavor is a tad lacking." He grinned and nodded, holding his cup out in her direction.

The phone rang, breaking the banter in the office.

Where in tarnation is Vivian? George wondered. He grabbed the phone. "Sheriff Logan," he answered. "Oh hey, what's that you say? Hold on now. Don't get your panties in a twist. I'll get someone out there right away to look over the situation. They should be there soon."

Hanging up, he addressed Sawyer, "You're on your own today. There's been a break-in or vandalism out at the Mossy Creek Ranch. I think you can handle it."

Pete and Ed exchanged glances. Sawyer didn't miss the exchange. *Was that a smirk on their faces?*

She ignored them. "I don't know how to get there,

George."

"I'll give you a GPS with the address plugged in. It's time you learned your way around these parts."

"Okay, I'm on my way then," she said, placing her hat on her head. "Any idea how long it will take me?"

"Twenty minutes to a half-hour, depending."

"On what?"

"Never know what you're going to run across on these back roads. Watch for deer and other critters. That's the main thing."

SAWYER ENTERED THE CRUISER, plugged the GPS into the cigarette lighter, and backed out of her parking space. She considered turning on the blue lights and hitting the siren just to make a statement to her grinning co-workers, but decided against it. She didn't need to lose her job for being insubordinate after only being there a few days.

She headed out of town, the GPS's monotonous voice telling her to take a left in 0.5 miles. Turning at the stop sign, she began driving down the frontage road. With ten miles to go before her destination, Sawyer took it slow and decided to enjoy the scenery.

Morning sunlight streamed through the tree branches and she could see the silhouette of the Tobacco Root Mountains. She rolled down her window and breathed in the clean, crisp, mountain air. A bald eagle, wings spread wide, circled overhead and disappeared behind the trees. Horses and cattle grazed peacefully in the pastures. This was heaven compared to where she had come from, and she was going to take her time to enjoy it.

The GPS broke her reverie: "Take a right turn in one mile."

Sawyer glanced at her watch and was surprised it had only taken twenty minutes or so, just like George said. It had seemed much further.

She turned onto a dirt road and continued a half mile before coming to a large open iron archway announcing Mossy Creek Ranch.

"You've reached your destination," the GPS droned on.

Sawyer drove through the archway and spotted several structures in the distance. Large stone walls flanked the driveway and beautiful split rail fencing enclosed the perimeter of the ranch.

Her eyes widened as she neared the house, impressed with the huge log cabin and wraparound deck. The sun glinted off the green metal roofing, and she squinted to get a better look.

A three-car garage attached to the building could only mean there were probably three new, sleek vehicles inside. Sadie told her that movie stars were constantly moving to Montana and Sawyer wondered if this place belonged to one of them. Maybe that hunk Bradley Cooper? Giddy, just thinking about it, she couldn't wait to see who it was and have a look around.

To the left of the house was a small duck pond complete with a family of mallards.

Situated away from the main house, she noticed a large red barn with towering silo, several outbuildings and what appeared to be a bunkhouse.

She pulled to a stop in the driveway and radioed George that she had arrived.

"How's it going?" he asked.

"I haven't gotten out of the cruiser yet, but I expect it will go okay. Why do you ask?"

"Oh, no reason, really. Call me when you're on the way back. 10-4."

"Will do. Over and out."

Sawyer reached over, removed her hat from the front seat and eased her way out of the vehicle. She grabbed her camera and placed its thick strap around her neck. Straightening her shirt, she took a deep breath, put on her hat, and made her way up the wide stairs to the front deck. She knocked on the door and took a step back, turning slightly to admire the mountains in the background. Now that was a view to wake up to each morning!

She heard the excited barking of a dog. When the door opened, a lively border collie with one brown eye and one blue eye came barreling out to greet her.

"Mabel, sit," a man's voice ordered. The dog sat at Sawyer's feet and licked her hand.

Sawyer looked up and, of all people, Jethro Byrd stood in the doorway glaring at her.

"Mabel?" She patted the dog's head. "Really?" *Why did she have to be sarcastic the minute he was in her presence?*

"You got a problem with that?" he snarled.

"No problem. I just never heard of a dog named Mabel. A guy named Sue, maybe, but not a dog named Mabel." Sawyer was doing her best not to laugh.

Jethro looked at her and shook his head. "I don't believe it."

"Excuse me?"

"I don't believe George sent a woman out here to do a man's job!" *Bet she won't like that statement*, he thought.

Determined not to let this man get under her skin again, Sawyer ignored his rude behavior. *Keep your cool, Sawyer. Do not rip his head off.* "George said you had some trouble out here?" She pulled a small writing tablet from her shirt pocket along with a pen.

"Yeah."

"Well, do you want to tell me about it, or are you just going to stand there all day ogling me?" *That'll get him.*

He had the bluest eyes she'd ever seen. The deep lines around the corners of his eyes indicated that he must smile a lot, although you couldn't prove it by her. His salt and pepper hair was gorgeous. She could envision running her fingers through it, and his teeth revealed a slight crossover of the two front ones. She licked her lips as she stared at his perfect mouth. She hadn't been able to get past his face to check out the rest of him, but one of these days....

"Ogle, *you*? You gotta' be kidding me," he snapped, even though that's exactly what he was doing.

Jethro fell quiet thinking how this redheaded witch was getting to him. He wished she'd never come here, because he instinctively knew she was going to be trouble.

"Well? I'm waiting to take your report." She licked her finger and flipped a page on her tablet.

I wish she'd quit that licking stuff. "Tell George I changed my mind. I'll handle this on my own."

"Fine, if that's what you want." She clicked her pen closed and put her tablet back in her pocket. As Sawyer was about to leave, she turned and looked at him again. "You amaze me," she said, a hint of sarcasm in her voice. "I can't believe you'd a let a woman stop you from finding out what happened to your property." Shrugging she said, "What do you have to lose? I'm here, so at least show me what happened and make the trip worth my while."

He smirked, thinking, *If I made the trip worth your while, you'd be flat on your back in the middle of my bed.* He could feel stirrings that he hadn't felt in a long time.

He stared at her and turned to walk away. Sawyer put her hand on his arm and he flinched as if she'd struck him with a red-hot poker. Jerking away from her, he went down the steps and started toward the barn. "All right. Follow me."

Sawyer practically ran to keep up with Jethro's long stride. "Slow down, will you?"

He smirked and hastened his pace.

What a jerk!

Someone had spray-painted a large white hexagon on the big, red barn doors. They'd cut the wire on the chicken coops and the occupants milled about pecking at the ground. Gasoline, siphoned out of one of the tractors, had seeped into the earth.

"Any idea who might have done this? Do you have any enemies?" *I'll bet he has more than a few.*

"Not that I know of."

Sawyer aimed the camera and began taking shots of the vandalism." I'm not sure what we can do about this, but I'll show these pictures to the sheriff. Do you know of anyone else around here who's been vandalized?"

"Haven't heard of anyone. There's a few other dogs with my men over at the bunkhouse and they didn't kick up a fuss, which is unusual."

Sawyer looked up at the sky. The clouds had turned a dark grey and were threatening rain.

"Could it have been someone they know?" She looked at the sky again as she heard the first rumble of thunder in the distance. Her stomach churned and her heart beat faster. She attempted to keep her voice light as she hurried the interview. She didn't want anyone to know how frightened she was of thunderstorms, especially Jethro Byrd.

"Hey, you're the deputy, not me. You figure it out."

"Well, you don't have to get all snarly about it. I'll go over this with George and get back to you."

She turned on her heel and started down the hill to the cruiser. The sky opened up. Large raindrops pelted her on the back and thunder boomed all around her. Sawyer took off at a run, her red hair flying behind her.

Jethro stood there in the rain watching her run, and felt those stirrings filling his body again. *What was it about her that made him feel alive again?*

CHAPTER 10

SAWYER PULLED THE CRUISER into Charlie and Sadie's driveway. Noticing a large red truck sitting alongside the house, she wondered who was visiting. Sadie hadn't mentioned having company, but then again, people around these parts just popped in without advance notice. It wasn't what she was accustomed to, but it was nice.

Entering the house, she heard voices coming from the kitchen. "Hello," she called.

"Out here, Sawyer. Come on in."

She went to the kitchen to find Sadie and Meredith at the table going over some paperwork.

"How did Charlie make out at the doctor's this morning?" she asked, grabbing a chocolate cookie from a plate.

"He's in the hospital," Sadie told her. "Meredith is helping me with some of these legal forms like Power of Attorney, Living Will, and a bunch of others. I don't know why we didn't do this before now. Guess we figured we were going to live forever."

"Now, now, Sadie," Meredith comforted, giving her a light hug. "You guys aren't going anywhere, not for a long time."

"What did the doctor say?" Sawyer questioned.

"Charlie is diabetic. His numbers were extremely high, so to get them under control he needs to spend a few days in the hospital. He's not happy about it, but that's the way it is."

"I'm so sorry to hear it. If there's anything I can do to help, just let me know."

"I will, dear, but don't you fret about me. You have enough to worry about with your new job. I have Meredith. She'll know what to do."

"I'll leave you two alone so you can get back to what you're doing. I'm going to head back to the office for a while. I have some paperwork to fill out myself."

"How's the job going?" Meredith asked her.

"Fine. I was called out to Jethro Byrd's ranch this morning." She made a face and rolled her eyes. "I don't understand him at all. Every time he sees me he growls like a stressed out tomcat."

Meredith laughed at Sawyer's description. "That could be his problem," she grinned.

"Whatever it is, I wish he'd be a bit friendlier. I've never done anything to him."

"Except annoy him, apparently," Meredith laughed. "Maybe he finds you attractive. Did you ever think of that?"

"No, but… yes, of course that's it," she agreed, grinning. "I'm such a ravishing beauty that he can't take his eyes off me." She paused. "What do you know about him anyway?"

"Not much, really. He's quiet and keeps to himself. He comes into the diner two or three times a week, but he's always alone."

"Hmmm. Well that makes me want to know more," Sawyer told her. *That, and he's the hottest guy in town.* "I'd best be getting back to the station. George will be sending a posse out for me. Just wanted to check in on Sadie and Charlie."

"Thank you, sweetie." Sadie gave her a hug.

"Why don't the both of you come to my house for dinner tonight, say around six?" Meredith suggested. "Dakota will be home and you'll have a chance to meet him, Sawyer."

"Sounds good to me unless I'm on duty. I'll let you know

later. Thanks."

"I have to go back to the hospital, but I'll be home by then," Sadie told her. "It'll be nice having someone cook for me for a change."

"I'll see you both later then." Sawyer waved goodbye as she made her way to the door.

JETHRO LAY BACK ON his bed, hands behind his head, looking up through the skylight, remembering. The storm was directly overhead, the blinding white jags traveling out of the clouds to the earth. Thunder boomed again, rattling the windows. Mabel whined and climbed up onto the bed with him. She bumped her head under his arm, wanting to get closer. Jethro reached out a hand and stroked her behind the ears. "It's okay, girl," he murmured softly to the shaking animal.

JETHRO BYRD HAD PUT in a 20-year hitch with the Marine Corps retiring as an E-7, Gunnery Sergeant, five years ago when he was forty. After two tours in the Gulf War, he became a Drill Instructor, (DI). Many of the young Marines hated him, but it went along with the job, if he was doing it right. He always hoped that being tough on the new recruits would keep them alive when they went into active duty.

A year before retirement, Jethro had fallen in love with another DI, Angelina Ortiz. Since the Marine Corps frowned upon fraternization, they'd kept their relationship a secret, except for confiding in a few close friends. Neither of them had ever married, so they planned to retire together, marry and start a family.

From the moment he met her, she had him hooked, completely. She was the most beautiful woman he had ever seen. Angie's hair was long and black, which she twisted around her finger when she was anxious. Her chocolate brown eyes twinkled when she laughed. And...she was built like a brick shithouse.

Angie was witty with a touch of sarcasm, and could make Jethro laugh just by giving him a quirky look. When she wrapped her arms around him and smothered him with kisses, the tough drill instructor became a weak-kneed teenaged boy. He loved her more than life itself.

One rainy night, after an evening out with girlfriends, she was on her way home when a drunk driver crossed the centerline, hitting her car head on, killing both drivers instantly. Jethro was home watching a hockey game on TV when the station broke in with a newsflash of the fatal crash. There were few details at the time, but his heart constricted when he saw the twisted vehicles, recognizing Angie's car.

He was beside himself with grief, moving through the following days in a robotic haze. Jethro requested to escort Angie's body to Arlington, and his superiors granted him permission.

THE FUNERAL WAS ALL pomp and circumstance, befitting the loss of a military officer. A hearse carrying Angie's coffin arrived at the gravesite. The Marine honor guard team secured the casket and Jethro and the chaplain saluted. The chaplain led the way to the gravesite, followed by the pallbearers who set the coffin on the bier and positioned the flag on top of it. Jethro stretched, leveled, and centered the flag over the casket before backing away.

The chaplain proceeded to perform the service. Jethro's heart was breaking listening to the words conveying the life of the one he loved so much. How could he let her go? How could he live the rest of his life without seeing her again, running his hands through her hair, kissing her and smelling her scent? *I might as well die myself,* he thought, as the chaplain droned on.

When the interment ceremony and benediction were

complete, the chaplain backed away and Jethro stepped up to the casket, presenting arms to initiate the rifle volley. Three loud shots rang out breaking the silence. Jethro winced at each shot. When the bugler played *Taps*, it was all he could do not to lose it.

The honor guard's team leader folded the flag and passed it to Jethro who in turn presented it to Angie's mother. She stood and hugged him, whispering, "She loved you so much." Jethro nodded, trying to maintain composure.

An Arlington Lady stepped forward and presented Angie's mother with a card of condolence. She was one of sixty-five volunteers who stood vigil at funerals where loved ones were present, or at those where no family or friends were present to render a final salute.

After everyone departed the gravesite, Jethro remained to watch over Angie's casket until it was interred into the ground.

WHEN JETHRO RETURNED TO the base, he put in for immediate leave. He spent the next three weeks in a drunken stupor. He didn't eat and rarely slept. When he did sleep, his dreams were of Angie, which made him drink more.

His friends came by and were shocked at his gaunt appearance; his color was poor with dark circles under his eyes. He hadn't shaved in days. They sat with him, offered him food and murmured condolences until he kicked them out of his house.

One morning his CO dropped by and demanded that he 'get his shit together.' "Look Gunny, you have one week before you report back to work. I expect you to be there, looking like a marine, not some bum in an alley. I know you're hurting, man, but you have to let it go, for now. Don't ruin your career, not at this late date." He left Jethro alone to think about it.

A week later, Gunnery Sgt. Jethro Byrd reported for

duty. He spent the remaining year of his hitch training new recruits, and he was tougher than ever. Behind his back, the men called him Hitler because they thought he was one crazy son of a bitch.

On the day he retired, he packed his few belongings, got in his car and headed for nowhere. He simply drove until one day he stumbled into the little town of Stony Creek, Montana. Deciding he was far enough away from civilization, he bought a ranch.

ANOTHER CLAP OF THUNDER and Mabel snuggled closer. Jethro rolled onto his side and buried his face in his dog's coarse fur. Remembering Angie was gut wrenching and tears slid down his cheeks. He would love her forever. After her death, he had made a vow never to fall in love again. He wouldn't be able to live through another loss like that. His decision had worked for him…until now. The deputy was awakening feelings in him that he thought were dead.

CHAPTER 11

DEPUTY MACKENZIE ENTERED THE office through the back door, laptop secured tightly under her arm. The acrid scent of burnt coffee filled her nostrils and she wrinkled her nose. Dirty mugs were lying on the counter along with spilled sugar.

They just don't care, she thought, shaking her head. Sawyer picked up the carafe and saw a black, gooey mess stuck to the bottom of the glass. Running warm water into the pot, she set it in the sink to soak. *It's a wonder this didn't cause a fire. Men!* She unplugged the coffee maker and went into the office.

"Hey, Sawyer, how did it go at Mossy Creek?" Pete asked, big grin on his face.

"It went fine," she lied. She wasn't about to let them know how Mr. Almighty Jethro Byrd had gotten under her skin. No way, Jose. She wasn't about to admit that. "Didn't you guys smell the burnt coffee?" she asked, changing the subject.

"Nope," Ed said. He didn't look up and continued working on a crossword puzzle.

"Glad to hear it went okay out at the ranch," Pete went on. "We figured Gunny might be in a sour mood since his place was vandalized." He laughed and jabbed Ed in the arm.

Ed's pencil flew across the room. "Cut the crap," he

barked, getting up to retrieve it. "Now, look. The lead is broken. Shit."

Sawyer shook her head at the bantering between the two men. "Who's Gunny?" she asked. "I went to Jethro Byrd's place."

"We all call him Gunny. He's a former marine, gunnery sergeant. Someone you want on your side if you're in trouble," Ed said.

"I didn't know that. He sure has a beautiful place. Someone spray-painted a big hex sign on his barn doors, cut some chicken coops, and siphoned gas from one of the tractors. Nothing earth shattering, but I hope we can figure out who did it before the vandalism escalates. Where's George?"

"He took Sadie up to Bozeman. He wanted to check in on Charlie. They've been close friends for years."

"Ed and I are going out on the road for a few hours," Pete told her, securing his duty belt around his waist. "Give us a call if you need us. We won't be far away. Vivian's not in today to give you a break, so if you're hungry, you can order something from Willa's café. Someone will bring it over, or better yet, you can go there yourself. Just lock up before you leave. We do it all the time."

"Okay. I have some paperwork to fill out first, but that's a thought. Any idea when George will be back?"

"Probably in a couple of hours," Ed answered.

Pete and Ed left, leaving Sawyer alone. She tidied up and made a fresh pot of coffee. As she was about to open her laptop to make out her report, the door opened. Sawyer looked up and smiled. "Hello, Doctor Webster."

"Hey, there." He took off his Stetson and held it in both hands. "Is George around?" He rocked back and forth on both feet sniffing the air like an old hound dog. "What's that smell?"

"That's the leftover aroma from Pete and Ed's coffee this morning. Is there something I can do to help you?"

"Actually, I stopped in to see you."

Sawyer pointed her finger at her chest and looked at Elliott in surprise. "Me?"

He cleared his throat and teetered on his feet again. "I was wondering if you'd like to have dinner with me this evening, that is, if you're not busy."

"I'm sorry," she answered, "but I'm having dinner with Sadie and Meredith tonight. Maybe another time?"

"Sure, that would be great. Guess I'll be going now. I'll call you."

"You do that. Thanks for stopping by."

Elliott let himself out. He waved at her as he walked by the window.

SAWYER LEANED BACK IN her chair, absentmindedly chewing on a pencil and thinking about what had just transpired. She hadn't dated in over a year after a turbulent breakup. She wasn't off men completely, but she wasn't looking either.

She'd seen the doctor at the diner one time when she first arrived, and he'd popped in the office a couple of times, but she was still surprised when he asked her out. She was flattered, but couldn't help comparing him to Jethro Byrd.

They were both tall and good looking, nice eyes, and Elliott had a great smile. She had never seen Jethro smile. Seems he was always growling and frowning when she was around. Elliott was a family man with a good career who was raising his boys. She and the doc were about the same age. Jethro was a bit older, retired, and seemed to be a loner.

From what Sawyer could tell, Elliott was kind, Jethro surly. While Sawyer really didn't know either man well, she surmised that Elliott was a good man. It seemed that Jethro had a dark side to him. Was he a bad boy, a player? Whoever he was, she was attracted to him. Damn!

Her belly grumbled. She threw her pencil on the desk and

decided it would be a good time to have lunch and meet Willa. She drew the blinds and locked the door after her.

As Sawyer walked down the wooden sidewalk to the Smokin' Barrel Café, many of the townspeople greeted her and shook her hand. A few of the women invited her to play bingo on Saturday night or go to church with them on Sunday morning. Stony Creek had five churches to choose from, but she did not intend to go to church. She smiled and thanked the ladies, telling them she'd see them soon.

Sawyer opened the door to the café and went inside. She took a seat at one of the small tables and waited for someone to bring her a menu. The aroma from the grill was mouth-watering, with smells of burgers, French fries, bacon and a hint of fish. She was definitely hungry now.

A large-bosomed woman in her mid-sixties with short brown hair rushed over to the table, big smile on her face. She wiped her hands on her apron. "You must be the new deputy. I'm Willa Mae Johnson. You can call me Willa or Willa Mae. I'm so happy to meet you. Sadie has told me so much about you."

Sawyer started to stand up to shake Willa's hand, but she wouldn't hear of it. "You stay right where you are, dear. I'll bet you're hungry. Can I start you off with a coffee?"

"That would be great. I'm famished," Sawyer told her. "It smells heavenly in here. I don't think I'll need a menu. I'd like a burger and fries, please, mustard and relish."

"Do you want a buffalo burger or a hamburger?"

"Ah, I tried a buffalo burger the other day," Sawyer chuckled. "I think I'll stick with a plain old burger this time."

"I'll be back with your coffee in a minute."

The door to the café opened and Doc Webster walked in. He looked over at Sawyer and smiled. "Hey," he said. Noting she was alone he asked, "Mind if I join you?"

"Sure, why not," she answered. "Have a seat."

Elliott sat down and smiled at her again. *Gosh, she's pretty.*

"Are you stalking me?" she laughed.

"I hadn't planned on it, but it seems like a good idea now that you mention it." He flashed her a grin. She noticed how straight and white his teeth were, not like Jethro's whose front teeth were a little crooked. *There I go comparing them again.*

Willa came back to the table with the deputy's coffee and set it in front of her. "Hey, Doc. What can I get for you today? Looks like you've already met the new deputy, you dog you." Elliott's face reddened and Willa laughed at his discomfort. She loved to tease and never missed a chance when it presented itself.

Elliott cleared his throat. "Willa, I'd like a BLT if you can stop laughing long enough to make it for me. Toasted, please."

"You got it, Doc."

"She's a prankster," Elliott told Sawyer. "If she can get a rise out of you, she'll do it. Be forewarned. One of these days you'll be on the receiving end."

"I can see that. I'm really enjoying the people in this town. Everyone is so nice and friendly, well most of them."

"Before long they'll become like family."

Before Sawyer had a chance to get Jethro out of her head, the door opened and he walked in. Her belly did that crazy little flip-flop thing again. He was wearing tight-fitting jeans and a blue denim shirt, open at the collar and cuffs rolled up. He was so handsome. She swallowed hard, looked down at his scuffed up boots and then back up to his face. Sawyer turned her head before Jethro noticed her eyeing him. She also didn't want Doc to see her ogling the cowboy.

"Hey, Jethro." Elliott waved at Jethro when he came in. "Care to join us?" Sawyer coughed, almost strangling on her coffee. She grabbed a napkin and covered her mouth, making eye contact with Jethro.

Jethro had observed the deputy and the doctor having lunch together the minute he entered the café. He shot a glacial look at her. *Didn't take her long,* he thought. *Damn little trollop anyway.*

"No thanks, Doc" he answered and took a seat at the counter. "Willa. Can I have a cup of coffee?" he barked.

"If you ask me nicely, I'll consider it, you grumpy old goat." Willa had a soft spot for the marine. For all his gruffness, he was a real softy inside. He'd help anyone at a minute's notice. "What's got you all in a dither?" she asked.

"Just having a bad day, that's all."

"Here's your coffee," she said, placing a mug of steaming liquid in front of him. "Oh, I added five scoops of sugar to it, hoping it'll sweeten up that disposition of yours."

Jethro scowled and blew into the cup. He wasn't sure if he dared take a sip or not. You never knew with Willa. She could very well have poured sugar in his coffee just to make a point. He took a small sip. Perfect. His eyes twinkled and he grinned at his friend.

Willa brought the deputy and Doc's orders to their table. "Enjoy your lunch," she said placing the food before them. Sawyer and Elliott had little to say during their meal, choosing instead to savor the taste of good home cooking.

Doc glanced at his wristwatch and finished the last few bites of his sandwich. "Gotta' go," he said, standing up. "The boys will be out of school soon and I don't want them coming home to an empty house. As I said before, I'll be calling you soon."

"That will be nice," Sawyer smiled. "I'll look forward to it."

Jethro had heard every word Elliott and the redhead exchanged and it made him seethe. *"I'll look forward to it,"* he mimicked in his mind. He clenched his jaws together.

After Sawyer finished the best burger she'd ever eaten, she went over to the register and stood waiting to pay her bill. Jethro was sitting on a stool with his back turned away from her. No way was she going to ignore him. "Mr. Byrd. How are you?"

Jethro's gut contracted and he felt that odd sensation

again. He could smell her perfume, a musky scent, and closed his eyes for a moment, mumbling something under his breath. He opened them and frowned into his coffee, then drank it.

"What's that?" Sawyer asked. "I didn't quite catch what you said." As hard as she tried not to, she snickered.

Jethro turned to look at Sawyer. Annoyance flicked briefly in his eyes. "Don't call me *Mr. Byrd.*" He mocked the way she said his name.

"Well, that's your name, isn't it?" she said sweetly, a mischievous grin on her face.

"If you have to call me by name, call me Jethro." Sarcasm dripped from each word. He stared at her uniform and reached a hand out toward her breast.

"What do you think you're doing?" Sawyer slapped his hand and backed away. "I could arrest you for that."

"Oh, please," he sneered. "Get over yourself. Maybe Doc is drooling all over you, but not every man in town is."

"Exactly what were you going to do then?" she demanded.

"I was looking at your name badge. Mackenzie. Guess I'll call you Mac," he spat, "that is if I have to call you anything."

"Oh no you won't! Who do you think you are? You *will* call me Deputy Mackenzie." Sawyer threw a ten-dollar bill on the counter and stomped out of the café.

"Willa," Jethro hollered. "Can a man get a refill around here?" He needed more than coffee to calm his nerves. However, he was feeling more alive than he'd felt in the past few years. He smiled as he thought about Mac.

Willa had been watching the encounter and she smiled. *There is definitely some chemistry going on between those two, but it looks like it might be a bumpy road.*

Sawyer, flushed and more frustrated than she could remember, hurried back to the office, unlocked the door and went inside, slamming it behind her. *I could wring his neck and watch his eyes bulge.* The image made her feel instantly better.

CHAPTER 12

"COME SEE WHO'S HOME," Sadie announced, grinning like a chessy cat at Sawyer as she came into the house. She grabbed Sawyer by the arm and ushered her into the kitchen.

"Charlie," Sawyer cheered, "you're home! I'm so glad to see you." She gave him a hug.

Charlie was sitting at the kitchen table drinking a small glass of orange juice. "I hope that's the last time I have to go to that godforsaken place," he grumbled. "They'd like to starve a man to death. When they did feed me, the food tasted like cardboard."

"Now, honey," Sadie patted him on the shoulder, "it wasn't all that bad." She leaned down and kissed the top of his head. "I'm so glad to have you home where you belong."

"Are we still planning to go to Meredith's for dinner?" Sawyer asked.

"Oh, yes, I called to let her know there'd be one more mouth to feed. She's excited to see her grandfather. How was your day, dear?" Sadie asked.

"It was actually pretty good. I had a call out to Jethro Byrd's place early, later I went to the café and met Willa, and then Doc Webster came in and we had lunch together. He asked me to go out with him."

"And you said…?"

"I said I would." She smiled.

"Well, Elliott is a nice man. You could do a lot worse."

"I'm not going to marry him, Sadie. I'm just going on a date. When do I need to be ready?"

"We'll leave around 5 o'clock. Dinner is at six."

"Okay. I'll follow you over in the cruiser. I'm on call tonight. I want to freshen up and then I'll be ready."

MEREDITH SET THE TABLE with her best china. She wanted everything to look extra special. She and Dakota had some exciting news to share with her grandparents and with Dakota's parents, Anna and Yuma.

Meredith had prepared a standing rib roast au jus, mashed potatoes and Brussels sprouts in a butter sauce for the main entrée. She hoped her granddad would be able to eat the meal without upsetting his diabetes. She had much to learn about his illness.

She heard the back door open. "I'm in here," she yelled. She heard the sound of boots as he made his way to the dining room. She grinned when strong arms encircled her waist from behind, and she leaned back against Dakota's familiar body. He nuzzled her neck and collarbone and blew gently into her ear. Meredith giggled and tried to push him away. He pulled her close, inhaling the scent of her freshly washed hair, and was instantly aroused. Meredith felt his erection against her.

"I love you, Dakota, but our company will be here any minute and we don't have time for this. I'll make it up to you later," she teased, "with a promise you won't regret."

He hugged her tighter and ran kisses up and down her neck. "It'll only take a few minutes," he whispered.

"Come on, Dakota," she squealed, trying to push him away. "You have to let me go, and you need to go wash up and get ready for dinner."

Dakota released her and turned her around to face him. "I'm going to hold you to that promise," he said huskily. He quickly lowered his mouth to hers before she could protest, and kissed her to the point that left Meredith breathless. Then he let her go, leaving her standing there weak-kneed.

"Damn it, Dakota" she stomped her foot. "You always do that to me." Meredith looked around for something to throw, but all she could see were her good dinner plates and she wasn't about to break one of those. She could hear his amused laughter as he walked up the stairs to their bedroom. In spite of herself, she had to chuckle. He sure knew which buttons to push to make her feel all giddy and girly. She'd never been happier in her life.

"YOO-HOO," SADIE TRILLED AS she opened the door to Meredith's house.

Tripp, Meredith's Border collie, bounded from around the side of the house to greet them. In true Tripp fashion, he attempted to herd them into the house. Directly behind him and imitating Tripp was Bill, Dakota's German shepherd puppy.

Sawyer accidently stepped on Tripp while trying to avoid the frisky animals. Tripp yelped and Bill ran the other way.

She leaned down to pet the dog's head. "Sorry pooch. They sure have a lot of energy," she remarked. "Are they always like this?"

"Always," Sadie told her, lifting her pie a little higher so Tripp wouldn't get the first bite. "He needs something to keep him busy."

Jethro's dog, Mabel, popped into Sawyer's mind. *Maybe what Tripp needs is a girlfriend.*

Meredith greeted them in the entryway. "Welcome, everyone." She hurried over to her grandfather and wrapped her arms around him, giving him a big squeeze. "I'm so glad you're home, Gramps."

"Sure good to be home, too," he said, a little embarrassed

with her making a fuss over him.

"Make yourselves comfortable in the living room. I'm not finished with the dinner yet so I'll be in the kitchen."

"We'll come help you, honey," Sadie said. "Charlie, why don't you go watch TV? Relax for a while until dinner is ready."

"Don't you start fussin', too, darlin'. I can take care of myself. You go sit with the girls." Realizing how tired he actually was, Charlie made his way to the living room, sat down in an easy chair and turned on the television. Within a few minutes, he fell asleep.

Dakota came downstairs and spotted Charlie in front of the tube. Just as he was about to say hello, he noticed the old man was sleeping. He quietly backed away and left the room. He heard the women chattering in the kitchen and decided to join them.

Sawyer caught a glimpse of someone coming into the kitchen and turned her head to see who it was. A tall, tan-skinned man with jet-black hair pulled back into a ponytail walked into the room. His features were strong with high cheekbones and deep set brown eyes. *This must be Meredith's boyfriend.*

He strode across the kitchen to greet the women. He leaned down, and planted a kiss on Sadie's cheek and gave Meredith a light kiss on the lips.

Meredith turned to Sawyer. "I'd like you to meet my fiancé, Dakota Morgan. Dakota, this is our new deputy, Sawyer Mackenzie."

Dakota smiled and offered his hand to Sawyer. "Pleased to meet you. I've heard a lot about you."

Sawyer shook his hand. "I'm sure you have," she chuckled. "It seems I'm the talk of the town. Pleased to meet you, too."

"Are you getting settled into your new surroundings?"

"Oh, yes. Everyone has been very helpful and I'm learning my way around. There's lots of territory to cover.

I've never been to Montana before so everything is new and exciting for me, especially the beautiful mountains."

"This is a nice place to live and work. I'm sure you'll do well."

"Dakota is a game warden," Meredith piped in. "The two of you may end up working together from time to time."

"That would be different," Sawyer said. "I never worked with the game wardens in Florida."

"It doesn't happen often," Dakota told her, "but there are times when we need the Sheriff's department to step in and give us a hand."

A loud rap on the back door announced the arrival of Dakota's parents.

"Mom, Father, so good to see you." Dakota closed the distance between his parents and him and gave his mother a hug. He and his father shook hands and leaned into each other for pats on the back.

"Looks like everyone is here," Meredith said. "Sawyer, these are Dakota's parents, Anna and Yuma Morgan."

They exchanged pleasantries and began making small talk. Sawyer noticed that Dakota's mother was Caucasian and his father Native American. The combination of the two gave Dakota his good looks, but he definitely took after his father's heritage.

The two men went into the living room leaving the women to get the meal ready. Charlie was still asleep, glasses slipped down onto the tip of his nose.

Dakota gently touched his shoulder. "Hey, Gramps. Time to wake up. Dinner's almost ready."

Charlie shifted in his chair, adjusted his glasses and rubbed his hand through his hair. "Guess I fell asleep. Hey, Yuma. Everything okay at the ranch?"

Yuma and his wife had worked for Charlie since they were in their teens. Anna took care of the house and Yuma managed the ranch. They had a small house on the same property and had lived there for years, raising Dakota to adulthood.

"Everything is fine, Charlie. Don't you worry about anything. If I need you, I'll be sure to call and let you know."

Sadie came into the room and touched Charlie on the hand. "We need to take your blood sugar before you eat your dinner."

He grumbled, but stood up and followed her into the bathroom.

"Dinner is ready," Meredith announced. She was excited about the news she and Dakota were going to spring on the family. The only downside was that her father, Dallas Banning, wouldn't be there to hear the news with the rest of them.

Everyone gathered at the dining room table, hungry and ready for the dinner Meredith had prepared. "Let's hold hands. Gramps, would you please say Grace?"

"Sure, darlin'." Heads bowed, Charlie began, "Bless us, Lord, and these Thy gifts, which we are about to receive from Thy bounty, through Christ our Lord. Amen."

Dakota held Meredith's chair while she took her seat. The others followed suit, placed their napkins in their laps and began passing the food around the table. Charlie caught them up on his hospital stay until Sadie shushed him.

"Sawyer, why don't you tell us about Florida," Meredith said. "I lived in the Keys for a few years, but did make it up to Kissimmee once when I went to Disney World. How was it being a deputy down there?" Small talk continued throughout the meal.

When they finished, the women took the dishes out to the kitchen. Meredith whispered something to Sawyer and she nodded.

The ladies prepared a pot of coffee and put the dishes into hot water to soak. While they waited for the coffee to brew, they went back into the dining room. Sawyer stayed behind. Meredith had instructed her to go into the pantry and retrieve a cake hidden under a Tupperware cover.

When Sawyer lifted the cover, she saw a small cowgirl figurine dressed all in white, from the hat on her head to the boots on her feet. Next to the cowgirl was a cowboy wearing black jeans, shirt, vest and a black hat. In the middle of the cake, they were perched atop a small bale of hay made of frosting. *Oh my,* she thought. *I wonder if this is the big surprise.*

Sawyer picked up the cake and started into the dining room. As she entered, Meredith and Dakota stood up, holding hands for support. No one else moved. They sat there gaping, as if they'd never seen a wedding cake before. Sawyer placed the cake in front of Meredith and Dakota and quickly took her seat.

"Gramps, Sadie, Yuma and Anna, we have some exciting news to share with you," Meredith squeezed Dakota's hand. No one said a word.

Dakota cleared his throat. "Meredith and I got married last month. Before you get all crazy on us," he said, holding up both hands, "we'd been planning this for a while. Then Charlie wasn't feeling well, you had a houseguest, and it wasn't the time to spring this on you. We never wanted a large wedding, so we decided to elope." Looking at the faces before him, he started to sweat. No one was smiling.

"We have one more announcement, and then we'll cut the cake and have coffee," Meredith interjected.

Dakota's parents and Meredith's grandparents looked back and forth from one to another, stunned at the news. There was more?

Tripp scrambled out from under the table and stumbled over himself getting to the front door. He was barking up a storm and wagging his tail to the point where it might fall off.

The front door opened and Dallas yelled, "Hey, little girl I'm home."

Meredith jumped up from the table. "Daddy, you made it," she shouted as she ran to greet her father.

Dallas looked around the room and spotted the cake on

the table. “Looks like I missed a party. What’s going on?”

CHAPTER 13

SAWYER'S PAGER WENT OFF and she excused herself from the table. "Sorry to miss the rest of the party," she said when she returned, "but there's been more vandalism out at Jethro Byrd's ranch and I have to go."

"We'll save you a piece of cake," Meredith told her.

"Thanks." She wondered what the rest of the surprise was, but knew she didn't have the right to ask, especially since no one else knew, and she wasn't family. "I'll be back later, Sadie. Don't wait up if it gets too late."

Sawyer glanced at her watch. It was seven o'clock, but she still had a couple hours of daylight before it got dark. Days and evenings were long in Montana and she loved it.

She made her way to Mossy Creek Ranch. As she drove along, she marveled at the mountains, which were turning a purple and golden hue in the evening sunlight. A few antelope were grazing in a field and patches of wildflowers blew gently in the breeze. She remembered that only a short time ago, the sight of an antelope made her giddy as a teenager before her first date.

Pulling into the gravel driveway leading to Jethro's house, she slowed down when the car made a bumpity, bump noise over the metal cattle guard.

She had never seen cattle guards before moving to Montana, and one day asked the sheriff what their purpose was.

"Metal bars are placed over a ditch and designed to be wide enough so that the animal's hooves and legs will fall through them and they'd get stuck," George told her. "Believe it or not," he said, "most hooved animals are smart enough to recognize the potential hazard and avoid them." Sawyer never gave it a thought that cows could figure out something like that.

She pulled the cruiser up in front of the house, put on her hat, and exited the vehicle. Jethro was standing on the porch, arms crossed, scowl on his face. Sawyer rolled her eyes thinking *here we go again.*

Mabel ran down the steps whining and wagging her tail in a greeting. Sawyer leaned down, petted her, and whispered in Mabel's ear, "Go find your ball." The little dog went bounding up the steps and back down again, dropping the ball at Sawyer's feet.

She picked up the ball and threw it a good distance, impressing Jethro, although he'd never say so. "I used to play softball," she said on her way up the steps. "So, what seems to be the problem?"

"Didn't George tell you, Mac?"

Jethro calling her Mac got under her skin, but she ignored him. "He didn't. Just told me to get out here because there was more vandalism. So, do you want to show me what happened, *Mr. Byrd,*" she quipped, "or am I supposed to guess?" *There. Tit for tat.*

Jethro had a difficult time not laughing; instead, he stomped down the stairs with Sawyer trailing behind. *He still has a nice butt,* she thought, wishing she dared to give it a quick pat.

Jethro couldn't help feeling that funny tingle again whenever the deputy was in his presence. She made him madder than hell, but she'd done nothing to deserve the way he was treating her. The last time he saw her she was in the café having lunch with Elliott Webster, and he had to admit he didn't like it one bit. He was jealous and took it out on her by being sarcastic.

"Do you know how to ride?" he asked.

"Ride? Ride what?"

"Ever heard of a horse?" he replied sarcastically.

"Well, of course I've heard of a horse," she shot back. "And no, I don't ride. Horses scare me."

"What are you doing in Montana then?"

"Isn't it obvious that I moved out here just to annoy you?" she spat.

Jethro's eyes twinkled in amusement at her feistiness. He liked that in a woman, and a slow grin spread across his face. He probably should back off and give her some slack. He didn't want her to hate him, especially when he had the hot's for her.

Sawyer quietly inhaled, noticing the incredible smile on his face. It was his eyes that struck her the most though. Crystal blue, but sad. She wondered what made him bitter and all bent out of shape most of the time, yet here he was grinning like a stupid schoolboy.

"What's so funny?" Sawyer asked.

"You've got a bit of a temper, huh?"

"It seems you bring out the worst in me," she admitted.

"That's one of my finer qualities," Jethro said. "Let's go to the barn and get the 4-wheeler. I'm assuming you're not afraid of those."

In fact, she was. However, she wasn't about to let him know.

"Why do we need the 4-wheeler?" she asked, scurrying along beside him.

"I'm going to show you where my property got vandalized. It's easier to get there on horseback," he arched his eyebrows at her, "but we'll take the 4-wheeler. Too far to walk."

"So what happened?"

"You'll see when we get there."

"By the way, who lives in the bunkhouse?"

"Why?"

"I'm only asking in case someone has a grudge against you. Seems like the perp or perps know their way around here and can get in and out without being caught."

"The men in the bunkhouse are all military buddies of mine. They've fallen on hard times. They're here to work the ranch and work out their problems. I'd stake my life that none of them would do a thing to hurt me in any way."

"Okay. Just thought I'd ask."

They reached the three-car garage and Jethro hit the automatic door opener. A 2014 shiny, black Chevy Silverado commandeered the first berth. A vintage 1970 Chevy Impala, dark red with two black stripes on the hood and trunk occupied the second. Sawyer was impressed with both. But, in the third stall, sat her nemesis. A dusty, beat-up Polaris Sportsman 4-wheeler just waiting for her.

Jethro jumped astride, started her up, and looked at Sawyer. "Are you getting on or not?" He patted the far end of the seat.

She looked at the seat, then back at him. "Oh, what the hell," she grumbled. Jethro leaned forward, while she threw her leg over and settled in behind him.

"You better put your arms around me," he told her. "Sure wouldn't want you falling off." He put the 4-wheeler in reverse and they shot out of the garage.

Sawyer held back a scream and grabbed Jethro around his middle. She swallowed hard fearing she was in for the ride of her life. She had the feeling he was mean enough to make this very scary for her, and imagined he was laughing inside at her discomfort.

Jethro enjoyed the feel of Sawyer's arms around him and her soft breasts against his back. He had the desire to lean into her to feel her better, but he controlled himself so she wouldn't be offended. A few times, he sped up just to make her hang onto him tighter.

Sawyer's thoughts were mirroring Jethro's. He felt so good against her body that she almost forgot her fears. The smell of soap and after-shave was intoxicating, making her feel warm all over. She wondered if he could feel her heart thudding against his back.

They traversed the fields and property with Mabel running along beside them until they were finally at the place where the damage had been committed. Jethro shut off the engine and helped Sawyer get down. Touching her sent sparks through his hand and into his heart.

"Wow," she uttered. "Lots of fences down and wires cut. Did you lose any cattle?"

"Not that I know of. I sent the boys out this morning to see if there were any strays. They're not back yet, so I can't be sure."

"You have no idea at all who could be behind this?" She was all business now, writing in her notepad.

"I told you I didn't," he said gruffly, still under the spell of her being so close.

"Don't be getting all huffy on me again," she said, pointing her finger at him. "I'm just asking a…."

Jethro leaned over and cut her off mid-sentence with a kiss, surprising the both of them. Sawyer didn't pull away and the tension between them was electrifying. She felt his tongue slide against hers and she opened her mouth a little wider to welcome him in. He put his hand on the back of her neck and pulled her closer while she wrapped her arms around him and held on for dear life. His mouth was demanding and persuasive and their lips fit together perfectly.

After a few insane minutes, Sawyer realized the compromising situation they were in and gently, but firmly, pushed him away. Their breaths were rapid and heavy and she turned so he wouldn't see the flush on her face.

He walked up behind her and turned her around. He put a finger under her chin and lifted it, gazing into her eyes. He gently traced the line of her jaw and leaned his forehead against hers before breaking away, placing a light kiss on her brow.

She leaned into him, burying her face in his chest. She was so embarrassed because she had let it happen, yet she never wanted it to stop.

"Hey," he said huskily. "You okay?"

"I'm fine. Not a very professional way for a deputy to act while on duty." She turned her head away from him again.

"Personally, I thought it was pretty darn good," he chuckled. "But if it'll make you feel any better, we'll get back to business. Just don't look at me."

Sawyer frowned. "Why not?"

"Because I'm afraid I won't be able to control myself if you do."

"Oh." Sawyer was as rattled as Jethro, but tried to maintain a professional stance as she went about looking for evidence. Walking around the broken fences and cut wires, she spotted something in the grass. From her jacket pocket, she pulled out some purple gloves and put them on while Jethro watched her. Leaning down she pulled some fabric from the ground and held it up to him. "This look familiar?"

"What is it?"

"It's a blue baseball cap. For someone to leave it behind, they must have been in a hurry to get out of here."

Jethro walked over to Sawyer and attempted to take the hat from her. She pulled it away from him and slapped his hand. "Don't touch. It's evidence." She placed the hat in a plastic bag. "Maybe George or one of the other men will recognize it."

"It's nothing more than an old baseball cap. There must be dozens of them in the area just like it."

"Maybe, maybe not. Let's look around in case there's something else we've missed."

Fifteen minutes later they walked back to the 4-wheeler. The sun had set and it was getting dark. Sawyer hopped on first and Jethro settled down in front of her. She put her arms around him again and leaned forward so that her face rested against his back.

Before starting the engine, he sat, smelling the scent of her hair. His body responded with a mind of its own. Before he got into more trouble, he leaned forward and turned the key in the ignition.

"Let's get back," she said, "so I can take this to the office. I *am* still on duty, you know."

"Whatever you say, Mac." He grinned and started the engine. They headed back to the house, ever so slowly, enjoying the feel of each other's bodies.

CHAPTER 14

"HAVE A SEAT, DADDY," Meredith motioned to a chair. "Dakota and I have some news for you. We just told everyone else before you arrived."

Dallas sat down next to Charlie and shot him a questioning look.

"Hang onto your hat," Charlie grumbled.

Meredith was fidgety wanting to get this over. Dakota put his arm around her for support. "Would you like some coffee and a piece of cake first?" she asked her father.

"No. What's going on that's making you so jumpy?"

"Dakota and I were married last month," she blurted out.

Dallas sat motionless staring at his daughter. Stunned, he felt like he'd been sucker punched. The last thing he expected was to learn his daughter was married. Why couldn't she have waited for him to come home?

He gathered his thoughts before speaking. "When you announced on New Year's Eve that you were engaged, I assumed we'd all be invited to your wedding." As he spoke, the hurt showed on his face and it reflected in his voice. He had dreamed of walking his daughter down the aisle and he felt cheated.

"I know, Daddy, but there are extenuating circumstances which brings us to our second surprise. I'm expecting." She squeezed Dakota's hand for reassurance as she glanced at her family for their reactions.

"A baby?" Sadie and Anna grabbed each other's hands and beamed. "We're going to be grandmothers!" Sadie crowed. They jumped up from their seats and ran over to Meredith. The three women hugged, cried, and the soon to be grandmothers plied her with questions only women would ask. The men stayed put with their mouths hanging open, except for Dakota who stayed by Meredith's side.

"Well, I'll be danged," Charlie said, slapping his knee with his hand. "There hasn't been a new baby in the family since Meredith and Dakota were born."

Yuma stood and went over to his son. "Congratulations," he said, slapping Dakota on the back. "You have many responsibilities now. I know you'll be a good husband and parent."

"Thank you, Father. I'm very happy. I have the woman I've always wanted and now she'll be the mother of my child." He lifted his chin with pride and smiled at Meredith.

WHILE MEREDITH WAS BEING congratulated by the women, Dallas had tuned her out, thinking how he had made mistakes in his lifetime, but was trying hard to atone for his actions. He felt Meredith and Charlie had forgiven him for staying away so long, but perhaps that wasn't true. Maybe she eloped so she wouldn't have to choose who would walk her down the aisle…him or Charlie.

After all, it was only in the past year that he and Meredith had reunited. When she left home at eighteen to get away from her mother and Stony Creek, there was nothing to keep him from leaving, too, especially with his declining marriage. For years, he and Velvet had a marriage in name only. The reason he'd stayed as long as he did was to protect Meredith from Velvet's verbal abuse.

Dallas walked out a few days after his daughter and never looked back. For twenty years, he had no contact with his family, although he had kept tabs on Meredith's whereabouts.

While on the road, driving a big rig, he learned that Velvet had died from alcohol abuse. He heard that Meredith returned home at the request of her grandfather shortly after her mother passed. Meredith was back in Stony Creek and Dallas wanted nothing more than to see her so he returned to town. After an emotional and bumpy reunion, he made amends with his daughter and Charlie.

Dallas, so caught up thinking about the past, only vaguely heard what Meredith was saying. *Wait a minute; did she say something about a baby?* He put his hand to his heart. *Well, how about that. I'm going to be a grandfather.* A wide grin covered his face, the hurt and anger disappearing.

MEREDITH HAD BEEN WATCHING her father. He was the only one who hadn't reacted to her announcement. "Daddy, are you all right?" Meredith jostled Dallas from his thoughts.

"I'm fine, honey. Just a bit in shock. One minute I hear you're married, the next I find out I'm going to be a grandpa."

"Are you okay with everything?" she worried.

"I'm more than okay." He hugged his daughter and gave her a kiss on the cheek. "I think this calls for a toast."

Sadie and Anna hurried to the kitchen for some apple cider and Meredith brought out the glasses. They poured the crisp, tangy drink into the flutes and raised them in unison

Dallas looked at Meredith and Dakota. "Here's to the new husband, and here's to the new wife, May they remain lovers, for all of their life."

"Here, here," the family chimed in. They smiled and the women wiped tears from their eyes.

"Now *I* have an announcement to make," Dallas said.

"You're not leaving again, are you Daddy?" Meredith asked.

"On the contrary. I'm back for good, but I have found a job. I've always wanted to be a tour guide," he said. "I was lucky and got a job up in Glacier National Park driving a Red Bus, which means I'll be gone for part of the summer and into early fall. I have to go up next week to start training. Going to the Sun Road isn't open yet and won't be for a few more weeks. This will be quite the experience for me."

"I'm so happy for you, Daddy. This means you'll be around more and home during the winter."

"It sure does, and I'll be here when my grandchild arrives. I can drive down on my days off. It'll be a lot different for us now that I won't be on the road anymore."

"This sure has been a day full of surprises," Sadie said. "I don't know how much more excitement I can take." She plopped down into a chair.

Meredith glanced at Dakota with a smile. "Oh, did I happen to mention that I'm having twins!"

CHAPTER 15

DUST AND GRAVEL CHURNED up behind Sawyer's vehicle as she drove into town. A young doe stood at the side of road watching her. She slowed down. Dusk was setting in and fireflies were taking wing in the meadows. She smiled as she remembered catching them and putting them in a glass jar when she was a little girl. She would watch them glow for a while, turning the jar round and round. Later she would unscrew the lid and let them go.

She noticed a *For Rent* sign at the end of a gravel driveway. Funny, she hadn't noticed it on the way out to Mossy Creek. She pulled over and peered down the drive spotting a small, yellow ranch house with a garage. *Perfect. I'll ask the sheriff about it tomorrow.* She wrote down the address and put the car in drive.

Recalling the afternoon's event, Sawyer, embarrassed by her own reaction to Jethro's kiss, squirmed in her seat. He'd taken her by surprise, but she sure didn't push him away. She had kissed him right back. *I hope he's not a kiss and tell kind of guy.*

A few years ago, Sawyer suffered a broken heart and convinced herself that she was emotionally unavailable, shutting off all men. Then, without warning, Jethro kissed her in a way that no man had ever done. It left her confused. The tension between them had been building, she could feel it, but it seemed to be more a hate relationship than anything. With one kiss, everything changed and she felt her heart soften toward the grumpy marine.

A rabbit darted across the road and Sawyer swerved to avoid it. Driving slower now, she could hear the night sounds of crickets, owls, and a lonely coyote. The last of the daylight was fading from the horizon silhouetting the mountains in the early moonlight.

Nearing town, Sawyer wondered when she would see Jethro again and what his reaction to her would be. She really liked him and hoped his feelings were the same. Maybe she wasn't as emotionally shut off as she believed.

JETHRO SLID OFF THE back of his black and white pinto, Domino, and leaned his elbows on the fence. Mabel lay by his feet waiting for her human to take her home. She was hungry. Jethro rested his head on his hands as he watched the sun slide behind the horizon and felt the cool evening air wash over him.

After Mac left, he had taken a long ride, trying to clear his head of the feelings that were making his insides jittery as a jumping bean. He couldn't get his mind off the deputy or the kiss they had shared. He'd enjoyed it more than he could have imagined. She drove him crazy with her independence and sarcasm. And that long red hair! He could feel the blood rush to his groin again as he remembered her scent and the feel of her body close to his. Kissing Mac made him feel alive again.

Jethro hadn't kissed a woman since Angie died. Thinking of her, he felt a deep ache of sadness, and suddenly he felt burdened by an overpowering sense of guilt, as if he had cheated on his dead fiancée. They had promised to be faithful to each other and now he had done the unthinkable. The feeling was so overwhelming he gagged. He threw his hat down, grabbed Domino's reins, and walked toward the barn. *I won't make that mistake again, Angie, I promise.*

One of the men from the bunkhouse had been sitting on the porch watching Jethro. "Hey, Gunny. Everything okay?"

Jethro nodded and raised his arm as if to say, "I'm okay."

The man went into the bunkhouse and spoke to his friends. "He's got it bad. It's gonna' be a bitch of a day tomorrow."

DRIVING PAST THE DARKENED shops in town, Sawyer scanned the street for anything amiss before parking the cruiser in front of the office. It was late, but she could see someone was still inside, probably George. She opened the door and Pete turned around in his chair. "'Bout time you came back," he teased. "Fresh pot of coffee in the back if you're interested."

"No thanks. It's been a long day and I need some sleep. I found something at Byrd's ranch," she said, showing him the bag with the hat in it. "Not much, but it may be something. Maybe not," she shrugged. "What do you usually do with evidence until it can be processed?"

Pete took the bag from her and held it up, inspecting it but not touching what was inside. "Hmm...."

"What? Do you recognize the hat?"

"Nope. Doesn't look familiar to me at all. We'll wait until George gets here in the morning and let him have a look-see. He'll most likely take it up to Bozeman to the crime lab. In the meantime, I'll lock it up in the safe." He set the bag on his desk.

"Maybe I will have that coffee," she said, running her fingers through her hair. "I should get my report written up so George will know what took place tonight."

"Why don't you go home and get some rest. You did a good job today. The report can wait until morning."

"Are you sure? I don't want to get into trouble. I haven't

been on the job that long."

"I'm sure. Take yourself home, get some sleep, and we'll see you tomorrow. By the way, you're about due for a couple of days off. I'll speak to the sheriff about it."

"I'm doing fine. I don't need a day off," she said.

"Sure you do. We all do or we'd burn out in a hurry. I'll see you tomorrow."

AFTER SAWYER LEFT, PETE fingered the evidence bag again, turning it over and peering at it intensely. The black hat had a blue fiery skull above the visor. A dark stain on the side appeared to be old blood. Pete's heart quickened. He picked up his cell phone and began to text:

U stupid SOB, you left your hat on Byrd's property! The deputy brought it in. Meet me tomorrow behind the library 7 a.m.

Pete slammed his phone closed and began to pace. *How in the hell am I going to get rid of the hat without Sawyer getting suspicious?*

The door opened and Sawyer walked in.

"I thought you went home," Pete said.

"I was on my way when I remembered something. Did you put the hat in the safe yet?"

"No, I was just about to. It's still on my desk."

"Good. I remembered that I hadn't taken a picture of it." She pulled out her cell phone and walked over to Pete's desk. She snapped several shots of the evidence and put her phone in her jacket pocket. "Thanks. George probably would have had my head if he didn't have pictures to go with my find. I'll get out of here now and go on home. See you tomorrow."

"Yah, okay. Bye."

Now what the fuck am I gonna' do?

CHAPTER 16

THE SMELL OF BACON tantalized the air as Meredith entered through the backdoor of the diner and into the kitchen. Involuntarily, her stomach churned and she could feel the bile rising into her throat.

She covered her mouth and made a beeline for the rest room. Leaning over the toilet bowl, Meredith gagged and retched, the dry heaves turning her stomach inside out. For a fleeting moment, she thought she might faint as a wave of lightheadedness hit her. *Please, God, don't let me pass out here*, she prayed, dropping to her knees.

When the nausea finally subsided, Meredith stood up and carefully left the stall. Leaning against the sink cabinet, she took in several deep breaths. Beads of perspiration stood out on her forehead and she wiped them away with her shirtsleeve. Holding onto the edges of the sink for support, she grabbed a washcloth from a basket on the counter, washed her face and looked at herself in the mirror. *What a mess. I don't think I'm going to like this part of being pregnant.*

Sandra was flipping pancakes when Meredith walked back into the kitchen. "Where did you go so fast?" she asked, turning to look at her boss. "Are you okay? You're absolutely green."

"I'm okay now," she answered. "Just a flu bug I guess."

The cook looked at her suspiciously. "Flu bug, huh?" She threw some sausages on the grill.

"That's what I said, flu bug." The aroma from the sausages began wafting through the air and another wave of nausea overcame her. Meredith dashed to the rest room again. It was worse this time. She was making loud, dreadful sounds and she prayed none of her customers could hear her. The door opened and she heard someone come in. *Oh no.* She barfed again.

Carrie peeked beneath one of the stalls. Meredith was on the floor, her feet laying sideways. This was not good. "Meredith, can I help you?"

"I'll be okay in a few minutes. Just a flu bug," she said, gagging again.

"Can you unlock the door so I can help you up?" Carrie asked.

"I don't think so. I'm so weak. Just go away. I'll be okay in a few minutes."

"Stay right there, don't move. I'll get you out of there." Carrie ran to the kitchen and grabbed the cook by the arm. "Meredith is locked in the stall and is too weak to get up and open the door."

Sandra glanced out of the service window looking for someone to help them, just as Dakota came in. "Thank, God. Dakota, hurry, we need your help," she hollered.

He grabbed the extinguisher off the wall and ran into the kitchen. He glanced around with a questioning look on his face.

"No. No. It's Meredith. She's sick in the bathroom and …."

Dakota was out of the kitchen and rushed to the rest room. "Honey, I'm here. Can you open the door for me?"

"I need to lay here for a while. Maybe I can do it later." Meredith had never felt so sick in her life.

Dakota went into the next stall, stood on the toilet seat and peered down. His wife had wrapped her arms around the toilet bowl, her head lay on the seat and some of her hair dangled in the water. "Sweetheart, hold on. I'm going to get you out of there."

Carrie came into the room. "What can I do to help?"

"Go get me a broom."

She ran to the kitchen, grabbed the broom and hurried back to Dakota. "Here you go." She passed it up to him, wooden end first.

He reached over, slid the lock open, and jumped off the seat to the floor.

Dakota opened the door and leaned over Meredith, trying to assess the situation. "Honey, could you sit up a bit so I can grab onto you?"

"I don't know."

"Well, would you try?"

Meredith stirred and when she did, another bout of dry heaves hit her. She moved her face toward the open bowl and made sounds that didn't seem human to her husband.

When she finally stopped retching, Dakota reached down, gently pulled her out of the stall, and picked her up. She looped her arms loosely around his neck. "I need to go home," she groaned, her wet hair slapping him in the face.

DAKOTA CARRIED MEREDITH INTO the house and upstairs to their bedroom. He laid her on the bed and she moaned softly, dragging the pillow across her face. He'd never seen her sick and he was scared to death. Rushing to the phone, he called his mother. "Mom, can you come right over? I think Meredith might need to go to the hospital."

"What's wrong, son?" Anna had seen Meredith the day before and she was fine.

"She's having a terrible time with throwing up," he said. "I've never seen anyone as sick as this. Every time she moves, she pukes."

A big smile lit Anna's face. "Dakota, Meredith is going

to be fine. She's having morning sickness, that's all. Go down to the kitchen and get her a saltine cracker. See if she can hold that down. If she does, then give her a little ginger tea along with another cracker."

"What if I can't get her to take it?"

"Tell her I said it will help take the nausea away. She'll take it. Trust me. I'll be over later with a mixture for her that she can take two to three times a day. It will help her sickness."

Anna got busy mixing up a nausea remedy for her daughter-in-law; one teaspoon mint juice, one teaspoon lime juice, and one teaspoon honey. She mixed it well and poured it into a jar. "This should help."

SAWYER AWOKE BEFORE THE alarm went off. She'd been awake every hour on the hour thinking about the evidence she found. Something about it bothered her. She rolled onto her side, scrunched up her pillows and tried to get back to sleep. After another fifteen minutes of twisting and turning, she gave up. Since she couldn't turn her brain off, she might as well get ready for work.

She dangled her feet for a few minutes and wondered how her day would be. She thought about the house she saw for rent and wanted to tell Sadie about it. It was time for her to get out on her own.

She hoped she'd see Jethro. The kiss they shared was still fresh in her mind. Just thinking about it made her feel all tingly inside.

She slipped her feet into soft, fuzzy, slippers and grabbed her robe from a hook on the door. Entering the hallway, she smelled freshly brewed coffee. *Sadie must be up already.*

"Good morning, sweetie," Sadie greeted her when she walked into the kitchen. "Coffee?"

"I'd love some, thanks." Sawyer pulled out a chair and

plopped down onto the comfy, blue gingham chair pad. "Do you have time to sit for a few minutes?" she asked.

"Sure. Anything wrong?" Sadie sat down across from Sawyer, frown marks creasing her forehead.

"Nothing's wrong, but I wanted to talk to you about something." She took a sip from her steaming cup before going on. "Yesterday when I was out on the job, I spotted a small house for rent that might be right for me. It's just off Mossy Creek Road." She took another sip of the hot liquid.

"You and Charlie have been so kind, but I feel it's time for me to get established. You know, put down roots, and get my own place so I'll feel like I'm home."

"I hope you know that you haven't been a bother at all, and we've enjoyed having you here."

"I enjoy being here, too, but I'd like to get a dog, maybe a horse, even though I don't know how to ride. The house I saw was a small ranch set back from the road, all fenced in, and what looked like a bit of land to go with it."

Sadie nodded. "I know the place."

"Do you know who owns it?"

"I'm not sure," she said, looking away from Sawyer.

Sawyer wondered if Sadie knew more than she was telling, but didn't press it any further. "Well, I'd better get ready for work. Thanks for understanding if I decide to move."

"Of course, honey. You don't have to hurry though. You have a home here as long as you need."

Sawyer gave Sadie a hug. "Thank you." She kissed her on the cheek. "You've been like a mom to me."

Sadie's eyes welled up. "Git on with you now," she said, waving her hand at Sawyer. "You'll be late for work."

SAWYER WALKED INTO THE station with a bag of assorted muffins and donuts she picked up on her way to work. Vivian was sitting at her desk knitting baby booties.

"Morning, Deputy."

"Morning, Viv. I hope someone made coffee," she said, tossing the muffins on the sheriff's desk.

"Ah, a girl after my heart," George said, putting his hand on his chest. "Fresh coffee's in the pot." He looked in the bag and took out his favorite, cranberry.

Sawyer poured herself a cup of the strong liquid and sat down in front of her boss.

"Did Pete tell you about the evidence I brought in last night from Jethro's?"

"He's not here yet. What did you find?" He pulled out his handkerchief and blew his nose with a loud honk. He looked at it before folding it together, and stuck it in his back pocket.

I could have lived all day without seeing that. Sawyer stood up and took a glazed donut from the bag. "I found a blue baseball cap with a blue skull across the visor." She took a bite of her donut.

"You don't say." George's mind was racing. The blue cap was niggling under his skin, but he couldn't put the pieces together.

"George? Something bothering you?"

"Where did you put the cap?"

"I left it on Pete's desk. He was going to put it in the safe before he went home."

"Well, let's go look at it." George stood, still chewing on his muffin and crossed the room to the safe. He squatted down with a grunt, turned the cylinder a few times and opened the door.

CHAPTER 17

DEPUTY PETE TUCKER PARKED his wife's black car behind the library. He told her he was taking it in for an oil change and would bring it back later on. He drummed his fingers on the steering wheel and his eyes darted nervously back and forth while he waited. *What the hell was taking so long? I told the dumb shit to be here at 7 o'clock.*

He grabbed the evidence bag with the ball cap from the glove box and threw it on the seat. *Damn fool, leaving it behind like that.* Fifteen minutes went by. The longer he waited, the madder he got. *I should have done the job myself, instead of sending that moron.* He lit a cigarette, rolled down the window, and took in a deep, slow drag. *I sure could use a joint.*

After serving two tours in Iraq, Pete Tucker joined up with Sheriff Logan as soon as he mustered out of the Corps at the age of 26. He'd overcome drug abuse with help from the sheriff, and finally settled down in his early thirties. He met Madeline Wilson at a dance and five months later, they got married. They bought some land and a few head of cattle, built a house, and had two children.

Thinking back, Pete felt his life had been going pretty well until that arrogant bastard Jethro Byrd moved into town, and later on hired his merry men, as Pete called them. Humph! Most of them didn't know a cow from a goat, but they called themselves ranch hands. Pete knew they were nothing more than a bunch of broken down marines hiding from society.

Shortly after Jethro came on the scene, Pete started having flashbacks. Night after night, he dreamt he was back in Iraq, waking exhausted each morning. Loud, unexpected noises startled him and he caught himself reaching for his weapon. He was becoming angry, frustrated and suspicious of everyone, even his wife. Pete wanted more than anything to get lost in a drug-induced stupor so he wouldn't have the nightmares.

George began to notice the change in Pete and one day called him into the office, as a friend, not as his boss. "Have a seat, Pete. What's going on? You having trouble at home?"

"Nope. Nothing's going on. Why?"

"Well, you seem to be preoccupied and jumpy. Does it have anything to do with Iraq?"

"I have dreams sometimes, and lately headaches, but nothing I can't handle."

"Do you know the marine who bought the ranch out on Mossy Creek?'

Pete nodded. "I've heard of him, but never actually met him," he lied.

"He helps former marines get back on their feet. If they need a safe place where they can talk or deal with flashbacks, he's there for them. I mentioned your name and he's up for letting you come to a meeting if you want."

"You did *what*?" Pete jumped up from his chair and stormed about the room. "How could you do that to me, George? Haven't I been a good cop, busted my ass for you when you needed me?"

"You are a good cop, Pete. I'm just worried about you."

"Well, quit your worrying. I'm fine." He stalked out of the office slamming the door behind him.

"HEY PETE. SORRY I'M late," a young male voice broke through his troubled thoughts.

Pete flicked his cigarette out the window and glared at the person peering in the window. He felt like punching him in the face. He opened the car door with such force that it caught his accomplice in the gut propelling him to the ground.

"Geez, Pete. Whatdya' do that for?" he asked, rubbing his midsection as he was getting up.

"Shut the hell up." He threw the evidence bag beside his unwilling partner in crime. "Take this and get rid of it. I don't ever want to see it again. I got another job for you. You still owe me, shithead. Just do what I tell you. Don't make me arrest you for what you did. Understand?"

The young man nodded. "What do you want me to do?"

"I want you to burn down that marine's barn. Tonight."

"He has horses in the barn," the kid said.

"I don't give a shit if his mother is in the barn. Do it!"

"Okay, but this is it. This is the last thing I'm gonna' do for you."

Pete reached out and backhanded the boy across the face. "Don't be telling me what you are or aren't going to do. You're mine and don't forget it. Now get the hell out of here." He kicked the kid in the ass.

The teenager picked up his bike and the ball cap. He looked back at Pete before peddling off. *I'm not burning down no barn and I'll never get rid of my father's cap. I gotta' go tell Ma.*

PETE TUCKER LET HIMSELF in the back door of the station. He grabbed a cup of coffee before going to his desk, stopping to snatch a muffin and warming it in the microwave. "Where is everyone?" he hollered.

"We're back here," George replied. "Seems like there's something missing."

"Missing?" Pete's body stiffened and his breathing

became more rapid. *Pull it together, Pete,* he told himself before joining the sheriff and Sawyer.

"I understand Sawyer brought in some evidence last night, a baseball cap with a skull across the visor. Said she left it for you to put in the safe, but it's not here."

"I remember her putting the bag on my desk, but when I went to put it away it was gone. Are you sure you didn't take it with you?" he asked Sawyer.

"Pete, what are you saying? You know damn well I didn't take it with me. We had a conversation about you not recognizing the hat, and you were going to put it in the safe for George to look at in the morning."

Sawyer was furious and knew Pete was lying. He was trying to get her in trouble to save his own skin. But why? What was he hiding?

"Are you sure you don't know what happened to the evidence bag, Pete?" He eyed his deputy with a questioning look.

"You accusing me of something, George?"

"Nope. Just wondering if you might have misplaced it."

"I told you. I never saw it again after Sawyer left."

"Okay then. We'll have to do some digging around to see if anyone might know what happened to it. I'll start with Charlie and Sadie since Sawyer lives with them. Maybe Sadie has seen it in the house somewhere."

"For God's sake, George. I'm not lying," Sawyer repeated. She didn't like being the brunt of someone's lie nor the possibility that George didn't believe her.

"I'll wait until Ed gets here before I do anything. Maybe he knows something. In the meantime, why don't you scout around and ask some questions, Pete."

"Sure thing." Pete picked up his hat and tossed a menacing glance in Sawyer's direction on his way out.

"Am I fired?" Sawyer asked.

"Hell no. I wanted to get him out of here so I could talk to you in private."

"So you do believe me?"

"I believe you. Pete's changed in the past months, but I can't put my finger on what it is. So, let's start at the beginning. Tell me exactly what happened when you got back to the station."

They sat at George's desk and spent the better part of an hour going over Sawyer's report, trying to make sense of what Pete had said and what may have happened to the evidence bag.

All of a sudden, Sawyer slapped her hand on the desk. "Oh my God, George, I just remembered. I took pictures of the evidence in case you might need them." She sprang from her chair and ran across the room to retrieve her phone from her jacket.

The phone jangled, interrupting their conversation. "Can you get that, George?" Vivian hollered.

"God forbid she'd have to work instead of knitting all day," he mumbled. The phone rang a second time. George answered, "Sheriff's office."

"Sheriff. This is Carrie Boone. I need you to come to my house right away."

CHAPTER 18

SAWYER WAS ON HER way to Jethro's house with news from the sheriff when her phone rang. She pressed the cell phone indicator on her steering wheel. "Hello."

"Is this Deputy Mackenzie?"

"It is. Who's calling?"

"Hi. My name is Nola Cummings. I'm the owner of the Gold Dust and Rouge hair salon in town, but I'm also a realtor. I heard you might be interested in renting the little ranch house on Mossy Creek Road."

Sawyer felt an immediate sense of happy anticipation. "I *am* interested. In fact, I'm heading out that way now."

"If you have the time, I can be there in fifteen minutes and show it to you."

She probably shouldn't stop, but it wouldn't take that long. "That would be great. I'll wait for you in the cruiser."

"Okay then. See you soon."

Sawyer continued down the gravel road leaving a trail of dust behind her until she came to the *For Rent* sign and pulled into the driveway.

Cheery yellow paint, white trim and a light brown roof with a satellite dish attached to it made up the exterior of the small ranch house. Two small columns flanked by river rock stood on either side of the etched-glass front door adding to the charm.

Split rail posts fenced in the perimeter of the home along with a gated front yard. Two large, empty wooden flowerbeds sat on either side of the front walkway and an Aspen stood tall to one side. Sawyer could picture herself filling the beds with flowers and vegetables. A side door led to a two-car garage.

She told the realtor she'd wait in the cruiser, but she couldn't help herself and got out to look around. Mountain peaks decorated the horizon. Behind the house was a porch and a large fenced pasture housing a small herd of animals that resembled Llamas. One of them came running up to the fence and made a high-pitched humming sound. She wasn't sure if the animal was welcoming her or signaling her to move away. The others stood watching nearby. They were beautiful creatures with fluffy, wooly coats; some white, some brown, others brown and white, and one was completely black.

The sound of gravel caught Sawyer's attention. She suspected that it was the realtor and she went out front to greet her.

Nola exited her silver SUV as Sawyer came around the corner. The deputy admired the attractive, middle-aged, slender woman dressed in a grey waist-length jacket and silk turquoise blouse. A large silver belt buckle accented the black jeans, and black boots finished off her outfit. The realtor's tousled chestnut hair, pulled up on top of her head, resembled a bird's nest, but, somehow, the look gave her an elegance that most women would admire.

"Hi, Deputy. It's so good to meet you," she greeted Sawyer with a smile. "I see you were walking around the house. What do you think?"

"If the inside is as nice as the outside, I think this is the perfect place for me."

"Well, let's take a look inside." Pointing, Nola said, "The side door over there leads into the kitchen, but I like using the front door hoping you'll get that 'wow' feeling when we walk in."

While she unlocked the door, Sawyer asked, "What type of animals are those in the back? They look like llamas."

"They're cousins to the llama. They're alpacas. Their fur is different and they're a lot nicer than the llamas. They only spit when they're agitated, and only as a last resort."

"Will they be staying on the property?" Sawyer silently hoped they would.

Ignoring her question, Nola said, "Here we go," standing aside so Sawyer could enter the home first.

"It comes fully furnished. I forgot to mention that."

When Sawyer entered the house, she smiled. The living room was small, but it felt warm and comfortable. "Wow. So far I love what I see." A large brown leather couch with an end table sat in front of a window with a light brown leather rocker to one side of it. Against another wall was a red easy chair with another end table, and its ottoman served as a coffee table in front of the couch. Colorful, Native American scatter rugs on the hardwood floors finished off the room.

"This is beautiful," Sawyer told Nola. "I'd give it my own touch by adding some personal items, but I couldn't ask for more than this."

"Let's go into the kitchen," Nola said, leading the way.

The small white kitchen had ample cupboard space, furnished with dishes, pots and pans, with a few antiques scattered along the top. The black granite countertops made a stunning contrast to the white cupboards and appliances. A small retro table with four wooden chairs stood in the middle of the room. Black and white linoleum in a diamond pattern covered the floor.

"Really, Nola. Can it get any better than this?"

"Well, it's a tiny house, but I think it would be perfect for you. Would you like to see the bathroom?"

Sawyer was already hooked on the place. If the price was affordable and the owner was agreeable, she would move in immediately. "I'd love to see the bathroom, thanks." She followed the realtor out of the kitchen.

The bathroom was quaint with a claw foot tub, a new pedestal sink, and toilet. The floor covering was the same as the kitchen. "This is lovely. Small but functional. How many bedrooms are there?"

"There's one master and another room which could be used as a bedroom, but is set up as a den for now. You can do whatever you want with it if you decide to take the place."

The deputy's cell phone rang. She looked at the caller ID and said, "I have to take this. Excuse me for a moment, please." She walked into the living room.

"Yes, Sheriff?"

"What did Jethro have to say about our plan?"

"I'm afraid I haven't gotten over there yet. I'm with Nola Cummings looking at the house that's for rent on Mossy Creek Road. We won't be much longer and I'll head right on out there."

"Call me after you speak with him. Good luck with the house."

"Thanks. It's nice and I like it. I'll call you in a bit."

"Okay."

Sawyer heard the phone disconnect. She walked back into the kitchen. Nola sat at the table with some paperwork spread out. "Everything okay?"

"I've got to get back to work soon. I'd like to see the bedroom and den and then we'll talk."

They entered the master bedroom. It housed a queen sized bed with a white metal frame, quite feminine compared to the rest of the house, as well as a large dresser. White nightstands held frosty blue filigree lamps and on the wall behind the bed was a picture of St. Mary's Lake at Glacier National Park. "Beautiful."

"Here's the den," Nola stood aside as Sawyer went inside. There were two chairs and a small television, but nothing else in the room. She glanced around and nodded. *I could get a desk and make this my office.*

"So, are you ready to talk turkey?"

Sawyer frowned and wasn't quite sure what Nola meant.

Seeing the deputy's expression, Nola apologized. "Sorry. I keep thinking everyone is from this part of the country, or is as old as I am and understands my lingo. Talking turkey means going over the rental agreement and deciding whether this house is someplace you'd like to live."

"I already know I'd like to live here, so yes, let's go talk turkey." She smiled at Nola.

They sat at the kitchen table and went over the contract. "Rent is $780 a month all inclusive. The owner would like the alpacas to stay, but if you object, he'll move them to another pasture. You would not be responsible for them. Someone would come by daily to take care of them."

"I'd like to have a dog that I can bring inside the house and eventually a horse. Are pets allowed?"

"Pets are acceptable. After all, we live in Montana where most people have a dog or some other animal."

"How much money do I need to put down to hold it?"

"Nothing. If you want it, it'll be the first month's rent."

"Are you kidding me? In Florida I'd need first, last and a security deposit."

"You don't intend on damaging the place, do you?"

"Of course not," Sawyer answered.

"Well, do we have a deal?"

Sawyer nodded and a smile broke across her face. "When can I move in?"

"How about tomorrow?"

"I'll get my check book out of the cruiser and we'll seal the deal right now. I'm so excited to finally be able to put down some roots."

While Sawyer ran outside to retrieve her checkbook, Nola dialed a number in her cell phone. "It's me. She took the place. I told her $780 and she could have a pet. Okay. We'll talk soon."

Sawyer rushed back inside and they sat down at the table. Nola pushed papers toward her to sign and went over everything one more time.

"Who do I make the check out to?" Sawyer asked, pen poised and ready to write.

"You'll make the check out to Cummings Realty every month."

"Who owns the property?" Sawyer asked, making out the check.

"I'm the rental agent. The owner prefers to remain anonymous. Is that a problem for you?"

"Not at all. I was just wondering." When Sawyer finished writing, she passed the check over to Nola. "You've made my day. I can't wait to tell Sadie and Charlie. Thank you so much. Oh, how did you hear that I was looking for a place?"

"Word gets around fast in small towns. Tell one, you tell everybody." Nola gave her a quick hug. "Here you go." She handed the key to Sawyer. "Welcome home. I'll be leaving now so you can look around again. If you need anything, don't hesitate to call."

"I won't and thanks again."

SAWYER SPED DOWN THE road toward Byrd's ranch. She should have been there an hour ago. She hoped George wasn't upset with her for house hunting before attending to her duties.

She pulled into the long driveway leading to the beautiful log cabin. Mabel ran up to greet her, barking and wagging her tail feverishly. Sawyer got out of the cruiser and leaned down to pet Mabel. "Come on, girl. Let's so go see the grumpy old man."

Thinking of Jethro, Sawyer's belly knotted up along with tingly feelings in her girl places. As much as she hated to admit it, she had a thing for the ornery marine.

She walked up the steps to the front door and rapped. She took a step back and waited for Jethro to answer. When he didn't, she whispered to Mabel. "Speak, girl, speak."

The little Border collie started barking and dancing around in a circle. Finally, the door opened and a less than amused Jethro Byrd stood in the doorway.

"Oh, you are home," Sawyer said, a slight grin on her face. "The sheriff sent me out to let you know what's been going on."

"I know. He called me. I thought you'd be here earlier. You expect people to hang around waiting on you until you're ready to show up?" he snarled. "It doesn't work that way around here, Missy."

"I'm sorry," she said, sarcasm dripping off her voice. "I didn't realize I had a deadline."

"What took you so long anyway?"

"If it's any of your business, and it's not, I rented a little house down the road. So Mr. Byrd, it looks like we're going to be neighbors." She flashed him a Saccharin smile.

Listening to her explain, Jethro watched how her lips curved, making him have the desire to grab her in his arms. He wanted to cover them with his own and leave her with a feeling as if no other man had ever kissed her. He wanted to keep his promise to Angie, but it was getting more difficult each time he was in the redhead's presence.

"Ah, could I come in and go over what we've found?"

"I suppose, but make it snappy. I don't have all day you know. Follow me."

Sawyer had never been inside the big, beautiful home and couldn't help but let out a small gasp when she entered the main living area. It was massive, with a stone fireplace covering one wall and leather sofas and chairs scattered throughout the room. "Well, I'm impressed," she said. "This is like something out of an HGTV magazine."

"A HG what?" he turned, scowling at her.

"Keep scowling and you're face is going to freeze like

that, you know."

Jethro stifled a laugh and coughed. "What was that HG thing again?"

"Oh never mind. You wouldn't know what I'm talking about if I tried to explain it to you." She glanced around the room again. "Mind if I sit down?" she asked, taking a seat in one of the big leather chairs.

Jethro grinned at her sassiness, and the lines around his icy blue eyes crinkled. *God she's beautiful.* He reached out and flicked a leaf off her hair.

She ducked and jumped out of her chair.

"Hey, it's just a leaf. I'm sorry." Her eyes were wide as saucers and Jethro could see fear in them.

"It's okay." Sawyer sat back down and slowly regained her composure.

He kneeled down in front of her and took her hands in his. "I'm terribly sorry." His voice was tender. "I didn't mean to spook you."

"No, no, it's okay, really. I don't know why I did that." She liked this softer side of Jethro Byrd, the man she was falling in love with, not the snarly marine who drove her crazy.

"Can I get you something to drink?"

"Nothing for me, but thanks."

"I'll be right back." He left her sitting while he went into the kitchen. He was a bit shook up from her reaction and didn't quite know what to make of it.

Mabel walked over to Sawyer and sat beside her. She stroked the sweet little dog on the head. Mabel flopped down and rolled over, begging for a tummy rub. Sawyer obliged.

Jethro came back into the room with a steaming cup of coffee. "Sure you don't want one?" he asked, holding the cup up to her.

"No thanks.

"Okay, what is it that's so important?" He sat on an ottoman facing Sawyer.

She could barely gather her thoughts as he stared at her with a stupid grin. One minute he was scowling at her, the next he was grinning like a fool. *God he's handsome.* "Well, we think we know who's causing all the damage. What we don't know is why."

CHAPTER 19

PETE TUCKER WAS WORRIED as he made his way home. His head pounded and his stomach, knotted into a ball, was killing him. He popped some antacids into his mouth to help ease the pain.

Was the sheriff suspicious of him or was he being paranoid again? His thoughts were all over the place. He was sensible enough to know his excessive worrying lately and irrational thoughts could get him in big trouble, but he couldn't help himself. It was that bitch, Sawyer, trying to get him fired. Women should be home where they belong and not parading around doing a man's job.

Damn George for bringing his name up to Jethro Byrd. Why would he single him out like that? He'd been a loyal deputy. He'd worked like a dog ever since George believed he could do better than end up a druggie and a drunk. Ten years ago, Pete sobered up, the sheriff gave him a job, and it had been good ever since, until that fucking marine moved into town. That's when the nightmares began again.

Jethro Byrd didn't remember Pete, but Pete would never forget the marine. When he was a young recruit, Gunnery Sergeant Byrd was his drill instructor. He was a hard taskmaster, brutal at times, and Pete hated his guts. What he remembered most was the gunny screaming in his face, demeaning him, and not being able to say anything back.

When he could speak, it was only to yell, at the top of his lungs, 'Sir, yes sir', or 'Sir, no sir.' When Pete's tour of duty ended, he vowed if he ever saw the DI on the street, he'd shoot him dead. Now, here he was on Pete's turf. He saw this as an opportunity for pay back.

Pete's temper steadily grew. The pulse in his neck began to throb and his heart raced like a hen in a yard full of roosters. Iridescent lights danced before his eyes making it difficult to concentrate on the road. Optical migraines the doc said. The pounding in his head was worse, and he finally pulled the car over to the side of the road. What he needed was a joint.

He reached into the glove box and pulled out a long, leather zippered wallet. Inside were his Zig Zag's and a small amount of pot. Small enough so he couldn't be arrested for possession should the situation ever arise. Pete pulled out a paper and held it in one hand. He reached into a plastic baggie with his thumb and forefinger and removed some pot, spreading it evenly along the middle of the paper. Bringing the two sides of the Zig Zag together, he began rolling it between his fingers, compressing the weed. Lastly, he licked the glue strip and sealed the paper.

Reaching into his pocket, Pete pulled out a BIC lighter and lit the end of the joint, inhaling a long hit of the musty, skunk-smelling smoke. Holding it in his lungs, he lay his head back and let himself float until releasing the pungent smoke into the vehicle.

After a couple more hits, his heartbeat slowed and the headache subsided. Pete opened his eyes. No more squiggly lights jumping before them. He felt better and his anger had calmed. However, his paranoia had not. He sat straight up and looked around, certain someone was watching.

SHERIFF LOGAN AND DEPUTY MACKENZIE pulled into Carrie Boone's yard. The front door opened and Carrie stepped out onto the porch to greet them.

"Hi, Sheriff, Deputy. Glad you came out as soon as you could. I have some troubling news to tell you. Come on in." She gestured toward the door.

George and Sawyer smiled at her and made their way up the steps and into the front room.

"Nice little house you have, Carrie," George told her. "Bet it feels good to be on your own again."

"It sure does. I thought I'd never see the day I'd have enough money to buy a place, but I did it." She grinned.

Carrie's husband, Taylor, died in a motorcycle accident and left her penniless. He'd abused her most of the years they were married and after a particularly bad beating, she and the boys moved out and in with her parents. The day Taylor was killed he was on his way to her parent's house to beat some sense into her. Alcohol, speed, and a large Ponderosa Pine contributed to his demise.

Eventually, life went on for Carrie. Reverend Storm Anderson, the most sought after bachelor in Stony Creek had admired Carrie for a long time. He finally asked her for a date and they'd been a couple ever since, living separately. Carrie was the happiest she had ever been. Until now.

"Come sit with me at the table," she pointed toward the kitchen. "It'll be easier to talk over a cup of coffee."

She set mugs on placemats and poured coffee into each of them. "Please, sit down."

George and Sawyer took their seats. "So, what can we do for you, Carrie?"

Carrie swallowed hard, embarrassed to divulge what her son had revealed to her. There had been so much trouble in the past because of Taylor, and now one of her kids was in a mess.

"Well, George, we have a big problem, a very big problem, and my son, Dusty, is involved."

George sat silently, waiting for her to continue. Sawyer took out her notepad and pen and smiled, urging her to go on. Only the hum of the refrigerator broke the silence until Carrie spoke.

"Okay." She took a deep breath and clasped her hands together, placing them in her lap. "You know there was vandalism in town a few months ago, spray painting the church, windows broken in some of the stores, and tires getting slashed."

George nodded. "Go on."

"Well, Dusty was one of the vandals. I never knew until yesterday, honestly. It seems that when the church was spray painted, he got caught."

George raised an eyebrow. "Who caught him?"

"Pete Tucker."

"Pete?" George leaned back on two legs of the chair and pushed his hat to the back of his head. He frowned and looked over at Sawyer.

Sawyer's face blanched. This was not good.

"What did Pete do when he caught your son?" George returned to a normal sitting position.

"He told Dusty he had a 'job' for him and he wouldn't arrest him if Dusty would do as he said. My son was scared to death and would have agreed to anything."

"What did he want him to do?" George remained pleasant and composed although inside he was feeling anger and frustration. His suspicion that Pete was a dirty cop had been justified. The knowledge nearly broke his heart.

"He wanted him to vandalize Mr. Byrd's barn and property and told him exactly what to do."

"Which was?"

"Dusty spray painted the barn, cut some wire to the chicken coops, and siphoned gasoline onto the ground. That was the first time."

"I think that's when I sent you out to Mossy Creek," George addressed Sawyer.

"That's correct. She's right about the damage."

"There's another time after that," Carrie went on.

"Dusty was ordered to knock down fences, cut wires, and run off cattle. He told me he didn't go near the cattle. After everything he'd already done, he said he didn't want to get arrested for rustling." She managed a weak smile.

"Is that it?" George asked. "You got that, Deputy?"

"I have, sir." She took a sip of her coffee.

"There's one other thing," Carrie said. "Dusty thought he heard someone coming that night, so he hightailed it out of there and lost his dad's hat in the process. As bad as Taylor was, Dusty loved him. Yesterday, Pete told Dusty to meet him behind the library. He threw the cap at him and told him to get rid of it."

Carrie stood and went to a closet near the kitchen. "Here, George." She passed him the evidence bag with Taylor's cap in it. "Pete ordered Dusty to burn down Jethro's barn tonight." She shook her head and continued. "That's when Dusty knew he had to tell someone and that someone was me."

George slid the chair back and stood up. "Where is Dusty now?"

"He's up in his room."

"Ask him to come down, please. I want to hear everything again, from him."

PETE PULLED INTO HIS DRIVEWAY. Exiting the vehicle, a small black and tan pup ran to greet him. "Get out of here, you mutt," he yelled, his foot landing on the dog's hind end from a powerful kick. The pup yelped and backed away, fear in its eyes.

His wife, Maddy, watched from the window and winced when she saw Pete kick the dog. She felt a trickle of dread and quickly stepped back away from view. She had prayed he'd be in a good mood when he got home, but it was evident her prayers were not to be answered this day.

Pete slammed the truck door and walked around the

house to the back door. *She'd better have supper ready. I'm starving.* He was always famished after a good high.

He yelled for his wife. "Maddy!"

CHAPTER 20

SAWYER PULLED INTO THE diner's parking lot. All afternoon she'd been craving a grilled blueberry muffin and a cup of hot tea. This had been quite a day and she wanted to relax and unwind before going home.

When she entered the establishment, the regulars greeted her with warm smiles, along with the wonderful aroma of good home cooking. The only girl working today, Julia Loomis, welcomed her as she came through the door.

"Hey, Deputy." She grabbed a mug from a rack and placed it on the counter where Sawyer usually sat. "Coffee?"

"Not today, Julia. I'm going to have a hot tea and a grilled blueberry muffin."

"It won't take but a minute. Have a seat."

Sawyer glanced around the diner and spotted Sadie and Charlie sitting in a rear booth. "I'll be back there with the Parkers," she said. She was excited to tell them her news and hurried to where they were sitting. "Mind if I join you?"

"Hi, sweetie. Sit yourself right down." Sadie patted the seat and slid over to give Sawyer room.

"How's your day been, darlin'?" Charlie asked. He took a sip of his decaf coffee and made a face.

"It's been busy. Do you remember me telling you about the little house on Mossy Creek that's for rent?"

"I remember we talked briefly about it one morning," Sadie told her.

"Well, I met with the realtor, and she showed me all

around. It's a great house, fully furnished, and there's a big pasture out back for a horse or whatever. Right now there's a herd of alpacas out there."

"Are you going to take it?" Sadie asked. She glanced over at Charlie, worry lines creasing her brow.

"I already rented it. Why? What's wrong?"

"Oh, nothing's wrong. We're going to miss you, that's all."

Charlie looked at Sadie over the top of his glasses which had slid down on his nose.

"What's going on you two? Is there something I should know?" The expressions on their faces troubled Sawyer.

Ignoring her question, Charlie asked, "When do you plan on moving?" He adjusted his spectacles with his thumb.

"I have a couple of days off this weekend. Thought I'd move then. It won't take long. All I have is my clothes."

Julia came over with Sawyer's tea and muffin and set them in front of her. She looked at Charlie and Sadie. "Can I get you anything else?"

"Nothing for us, thanks," Sadie told her.

Doc Webster came in, spotted them and made his way to their booth. "Mind if I sit down?" Charlie scooted over so Elliott could sit. He flashed a grin at Sawyer. "Hey, how have you been? Haven't seen you around much."

A slow smile spread across her face. "I've been fine. Still learning my way around. How about you?"

Charlie was about to say something when Sadie kicked him under the table.

"Oww! What'd you do that for?" He leaned down and rubbed his shin.

"Sorry to interrupt the conversation, but we were just about to leave. If you'll excuse us, we have to get going. Come on, Charlie." Sadie glanced at Sawyer. "We'll see you at home later?"

Sawyer nodded and stood to let Sadie out. The doc did

the same for Charlie. When they sat down again, Elliott reached over and took Sawyer's hands. "I've missed you. I'd like to take you out to dinner. That is, if you'll go with me."

The door opened and Jethro walked into the diner. The first thing he saw was Elliott holding *her* hands, and jealousy gripped him like a vise. A muscle twitched in his jaw and he shot her a contemptuous glare. He strode toward the counter and dropped heavily onto a stool.

"Hey there, Gunny. Coffee?" Julia asked.

"Yup."

She poured him a mug and placed it in front of him. "You want something to eat?"

"Nope."

Julia was certain she heard a growl come out of him. "Well, let me know if you want anything else." *He sure has a thorn in his drawers today,* she thought as she filled the catsup bottle.

Sawyer pulled her hands from Elliott's and glanced at Jethro. As if he could feel her eyes on him, he turned and gave her a defiant stare, causing her to turn away. If looks could kill, she'd be dead. Her heart gave a painful little tug. She felt such a strong attraction between them, but other than the one kiss, he'd never asked her out or suggested they take the attraction further.

Jethro was doing a slow burn. He felt like a pressure cooker about to explode and he could swear steam was coming out of his ears. Indecision gnawed at his belly and he hated feeling this way. He could either pursue a relationship with her or not. It was that simple. So why was he being all stupid and blaming everything on her?

"Something wrong?" Elliott asked Sawyer.

She looked at him and smiled. "No. There's nothing wrong, and yes, I would like to go on that date with you."

Doc's face lit up with her unexpected answer. "That's great! How about Saturday?"

"I'll be moving on Saturday and want to get settled

over the weekend. Maybe next week?"

"Where are you moving to? I thought you liked living with the Parkers."

"I do. It's just that I want my own place where I can put down some roots. I've been living out of a suitcase, and it'll be nice to have a home."

"I could help you move if you'd like," he offered. "The boys are good at helping, too."

"I don't have much. I'd really rather do it myself, but thanks for the offer." Sawyer took a sip of her cold tea and grimaced. She never had the chance to eat her muffin with all the talking and scowling going on. She looked over at Jethro again who seemed to be grumbling into his coffee cup.

IN ANTICIPATION OF HER move, the week seemed to drag by, one slow day after another. Saturday couldn't come soon enough for Sawyer. She kept busy with her job, although nothing much was going on in Stony Creek the past few days, making her workweek seem even longer. In between her duties, she made the rounds to the utilities' offices and put them in her name, and, lastly, went to the post office to fill out a permanent change of address. She finally had a place to call home.

Friday night she packed her few belongings into her one suitcase. Sadie fussed over her, unhappy that Sawyer was moving out. "You don't have to leave, you know. You have a perfectly good home right here with Charlie and me." Wiping a tear from her eye, she thrust a cardboard box at Sawyer filled with sheets, blankets, towels, and paper items. "I thought these might help."

"Thank you, Sadie." She gave the motherly woman a warm hug. She wanted to tell Sadie, who had treated her like a daughter, that she didn't have to give her anything, that she was going to be fine, but Sawyer knew she would have been insulted had she said so.

Charlie gave her a small desk that had been stored in his attic for years. "This old thing has been hanging around gathering dust. Thought you might be able to use it in your office." Sawyer gave him a hearty hug. He cleared his throat, blew his nose into his handkerchief, and went outside.

"He loves you like a granddaughter, sweetie."

Sawyer was feeling guiltier by the minute. She'd spent the last three months under the wings of these two wonderful people who had welcomed her warmly into their home, but it was time to try her own wings and see where they would take her.

SATURDAY! MOVING DAY! SAWYER was as excited as a five-year-old waiting for Santa on Christmas Eve. Her eyes popped open like two window shades as a burst of morning sun spilled in through the bedroom window. Laying there, she glanced around, knowing this would be the last time she would awaken in this room. She could smell the coffee brewing and heard the sounds of Sadie moving about the kitchen. Unexpectedly, tears filled her eyes and she felt a sense of sadness. These people had been so good to her it would be hard to say good-bye. *For heaven's sake, Sawyer, you're only moving down the road, not to Timbuktu!*

Sawyer got out of bed and threw on a pair of jeans, white cotton t-shirt with the words, 'Chocolate doesn't ask questions. Chocolate understands.' She pulled on the new boots she purchased once she knew she was getting the house. She couldn't go walking through pastures in sneakers or sandals. She ran a brush through her copper hair before taking the stairs two at a time to reach the kitchen.

Sadie was at the stove scrambling eggs in one pan and frying ham and potatoes in another. Four slices of bread were waiting to be toasted, and three small glasses of orange juice were sitting on the table.

"Morning, Sadie," Sawyer said, leaning in to give her a

quick peck on the cheek.

"Good morning, sweetie. Coffee's ready and your juice is on the table."

"Thanks," Sawyer said, reaching for a cup. "I hope you're not going to all this trouble for me." She poured the coffee and looked out the kitchen window. "I'm going to miss this view." The high white-capped peaks of the Tobacco Roots glistened in the sunshine and light puffy clouds floated high in the sky.

"You're going to have your own view when you move into your house," Sadie told her. "It'll be just as nice as ours and you'll come to love it. Time for us to have a bite and then we'll help you move."

"I don't have that much, Sadie. I can do it myself."

"Hogwash. I won't have you moving out of here until I know you have a decent place. There'll be no more talk about it." She wiped her hands on her apron and walked to the staircase. "Charlie! Time to eat."

"Be right there, darlin'."

CHARLIE LOADED UP THE old red truck with the desk and several boxes, along with Sawyer's one suitcase. When the items were secure, he jumped into the driver's seat and headed down the driveway. Sawyer and Sadie followed behind in the cruiser. The move to 1696 Mossy Creek Road went smoothly.

Sadie gave instant approval as soon as she entered the house. "This is a doll house, honey. You'll be so happy here. Look at the view. Beautiful!"

Sawyer smiled with relief. It didn't take more than an hour to put her things away. Sadie made her bed and Charlie placed the desk in a corner of the den while Sawyer was busy with her personal items.

"Well, guess we're done here for now," Sadie said, tears in her eyes.

"Don't you dare cry," Sawyer admonished. "I promise to invite you to supper real soon."

Sadie wiped her eyes and Charlie patted Sawyer on the back. "We'd best be going now. Call if you need anything, anything at all."

"I sure will. Don't worry about me. How about a group hug before you go."

They grinned and moved into each other, hugging and laughing, before breaking apart.

"See you soon," Sawyer said, waving goodbye.

After they left, Sawyer opened the fridge to get a bottle of water. Empty! *Way to go, Sawyer. You thought of everything but food. I'm surprised Sadie wasn't all over this.*

IT HAD STARTED TO drizzle when Sawyer headed to town for groceries, but by the time she returned home it was coming down in sheets. *So much for a sunny day.* Rumbles of thunder made her stomach churn. Her one concern was getting in the house before the weather turned into a full-blown thunderstorm.

She ran to the side door and pulled her key out of her pocket. Balancing a bag of groceries in one arm while trying to unlock the side door with the other, the soggy brown paper bag broke and her food went flying everywhere. "Dammit!" She tried to catch some of the falling food items, but in her attempt lost her footing on the doorstep. She tumbled backward and landed on her backside in the driveway.

Jethro was on his way home from town when he spotted Sawyer. Her groceries were flying in the air before she hit the ground. His heart clenched in his chest. He hit the brakes and fishtailed into her yard. He threw the truck into park, jumped out and ran over to her. She was lying in a large puddle with the rain beating down on her face. "You okay?"

"Hell no, I'm not okay," she yelled, looking up at him. "Do I look okay to you?"

He gently moved her arms and legs, and felt her ribs, making sure nothing was broken before he moved her.

She shoved his hands away. "Get your hands off me, you pervert!" She was mad, but enjoyed feeling his hands on her body at the same time.

He grinned and pulled her to a sitting position.

"Are you hurt?"

"No, I'm not hurt," she hissed. Her teeth were chattering from being wet and cold. "You want to help me up or are you just going to stand there playing twenty questions?"

Jethro's eyes twinkled in amusement. *God, I think I might be falling in love with this woman.* He held out a hand to her. "Grab on. I hope you're not a heavy weight," he said with feigned sarcasm as he hauled her to her feet.

Sawyer wanted to respond to the Neanderthal, but the only things she could think to say were less than lady-like. She knew she must look like a drowned rat. "You going to help me pick this stuff up?" She slung a couple bottles of water at him.

He caught them and flashed that dumb grin at her again. Her girly parts went all wiggly when he did that.

Thrusting the bottles under his arm he asked, "Where's your key?"

"I don't know," she grumbled. "Maybe it's still in the door?"

Jethro went up to the door and saw the key dangling from the keyhole. "Yup, got it right here. Want me to open it?" he teased.

"Oh, for the love of God, Jethro…open the damn door!"

He burst out laughing. He was soaking wet by now, but was having one of the best days he'd had in a long time.

CHAPTER 21

"NICE PLACE," JETHRO SAID as he helped a sopping wet Sawyer into the tiny kitchen. She was mumbling under her breath. Pervert, asshole, and a few other choice words bounced off his ears as she slammed plastic water bottles and cans onto the table. He didn't want to laugh, but she was making it nearly impossible. "Can I help?" he dared ask.

Sawyer shot him a look that clearly said eat shit and die.

"Where's the bathroom?"

"In there," she snarled, pointing the way. She grabbed a paper towel and began wiping the water and mud off her purchases.

Jethro went into the bathroom and grabbed a large, yellow towel hanging on a rack. He went back to the kitchen and offered it to her. "Here. Wipe yourself off and you'll feel a little better."

"Freakin' moron," she muttered, grabbing the towel from his hand and furiously drying her hair. She glanced at Jethro from under the towel and he was grinning like an idiot. She felt like punching him and kissing him at the same time.

"Why don't you let me take care of the groceries while you change out of those wet clothes?" He couldn't help himself so he threw her a barb. "You're a total mess."

"Oh!" she hollered, clenching her fists and stomping off to her bedroom.

Jethro wiped off the bottles and cans thinking of her disrobing in the other room. He could feel the blood rush to his groin and tried to think of something else. She would *not* be happy when she came out of the room if he was standing there with an erection.

While Sawyer was changing out of her wet clothes, her thoughts turned to the handsome gunny sergeant standing in her kitchen. One minute she wanted to devour him and the next she wanted to kill him. No one had ever made her emotions shoot up and down the way he did. He seemed to enjoy needling her, egging her until she blew up and then he laughed. Her stomach fluttered every time she thought of him. She knew she was in dangerous territory, but she couldn't seem to get him out of her mind.

"You okay in there?" he asked. "You're taking long enough. Don't make me come in there after you."

"You stay put," she ordered. "I'll be right out."

She could swear she heard him laugh. She pulled on a pair of panties and threw on her light blue fuzzy bathrobe. Wrapping a towel around her hair, she walked out of the room.

He was standing just outside her bedroom door, arms crossed and leaning against the wall. He looked so fine she could feel her knees wobble. His denim shirt clung to his body and she could see ripples of his muscles through the wet fabric. She had to control herself not to reach out and touch him. His jeans hugged his legs making them look lean and hard. Her girl parts started dancing.

"You better get home," she said, not daring to look into his eyes for fear he could tell what she was thinking. "You're soaking wet and leaving puddles on my floors."

Jethro took a step forward and looked at her for a long, meaningful moment before slipping his arms around her and pulling her to him. She didn't resist. He could feel her breasts press against his chest as she stood on tiptoe and clasped her hands behind his head. Neither of them uttered a word. Jethro groaned down deep in his throat as she pulled his head toward her. He covered her mouth in a powerful kiss and she answered with a need that matched his own. She could feel his hardness as his tongue slid against hers. His hand traveled toward her naked breast, stopping just short of touching her. He didn't want to rush things or scare her off, but she pressed herself harder into him, urging him on.

There was a knock at the door. "Hey, you okay in here?" the sheriff hollered as he knocked one more time before letting himself in.

At the sound, Sawyer's eyes opened wide, she gulped and pushed Jethro away from her so violently that he crashed smack, dab into the wall.

"Damn," he said, rubbing the back of his head. He'd never lost an erection quite that quickly before, and just when things were heating up.

"Sawyer!" George hollered. "Are you alright?"

"I'm fine, Sheriff," she said. "I'll be right out. *You* stay right here," she hissed at Jethro, jabbing him in the chest with her index finger. "I don't want him to see you." She pulled her robe tight and ran her hands through her mussed up hair.

"My truck is in the yard. Don't you think he's going to know I'm here?" Jethro whispered.

"Shit! George. I'll be right there," she called to the sheriff again. Sawyer ran to her bedroom to pull on some clothes.

Jethro waited a full minute before walking to the kitchen where George was standing. He thought it was stupid to remain hidden, so decided to confront the situation and see what would happen. "Hey, Sheriff."

George nodded. "Jethro. Didn't expect to see you here."

"Well, the deputy took a spill off the doorstep and I helped her into the house."

"Is she hurt?" He passed Jethro a package of hamburger. "Found this on the ground."

"She's fine. I think her pride's a little damaged, but nothing to worry about."

"Hmmm. So you were just driving by at the exact time she fell?"

"Yup. That's what happened, Sheriff. Lucky for her."

George raised his eyebrows and was about to say more when Sawyer walked into the room. "Hi, George. What brings you out this way?"

"I was heading to Jethro's to talk to him when I spotted his truck in your yard. His door was wide open as if something had happened."

"Oh, crap," Jethro said. "Probably the inside of the cab is one wet mess."

"Well, sorr-eeee," Sawyer dragged out the word. "I'll try not to fall next time. Who asked you to stop anyway?"

"Can I get you something to drink?" she asked the sheriff.

"No thanks. Jethro, you on your way home?"

"I guess I'm no longer needed here, so yeah, I'm going home."

"Mind if I follow along? I have a few things I want to discuss."

Sawyer felt her face redden and she hoped the discussion was not going to be about her.

"I'm glad you're okay," Jethro said. "I'll check in with you later."

"I'm fine. That won't be necessary." *Now why did I say that?*

"Whatever. Ready, Sheriff?"

The two men left together leaving Sawyer alone to think about what had transpired. She wanted him to check in on her later, but she had to be mouthy and tell him not to. She knew she was falling in love, but before she could take this further, she needed to talk to Elliott.

The kind, young doctor had let Sawyer know, on more than one occasion, that he was ready to start dating after his divorce. She'd had lunch with him once, but it wasn't an official date, just a casual encounter. Now he was asking her to go out with him. Not wanting to mislead him, she thought she should let him know she wasn't available. She might be letting a good guy get away, but she was willing to take that chance.

JETHRO AND GEORGE SAT in front of the fireplace listening to the fire hiss and snap as they swigged a beer. "What's on your mind, George?"

"As much as I hate to say it, we know who's been vandalizing your property."

"You going to fill me in?" Mabel whined and nudged her nose under Jethro's arm. Absent mindedly, he reached down and stroked the little dog on her head and back. "Lie down, Mabel," he told her. She plopped down on Jethro's feet with a loud sigh.

George laughed. "Just like a woman. Has to have the last word."

Jethro nodded and smiled. "So tell me what's going on."

"Dusty Boone has been the one causing the damage. However, he's not the real perp. Pete Tucker is."

"Pete Tucker. Your deputy? Why?"

"I'm not exactly sure, but I'm thinking maybe you can help. I'm going to make it mandatory for him to attend your meetings to see if he can work through what's bothering him. If not, I'm going to have to fire him. I don't want to do that because of his wife and family, but he has some major issues that need addressing. I know it's asking a lot under the circumstances, but are you willing to help?"

"What's the kid got to do with it?"

"He vandalized the church after his father was killed in the motorcycle accident last year. Acting out, I guess. Pete caught him. Told him if he'd do a job for him, he wouldn't arrest him. Dusty didn't know what he had to do, so he went along with it." George took a pull off his beer and continued. "The last straw was when Pete told Dusty to burn down your barn. That's when he told his mother and she called me."

"It's going to be pretty hard not to want to punch him in the chops for what he's already done, but I understand post-traumatic stress disorder, and I won't turn my back on someone who needs to talk things through. You mentioned he was a former marine."

"Yes, he is. He was a drunk and a druggie when he got out, but he cleaned himself up and I hired him. He's been a good cop until the last couple of years. That's when I started to notice a change in him. He won't talk about it. Says nothing is wrong."

"You get him here and I won't turn him away," Jethro said. "We meet the third Thursday of the month at 7 o'clock. More often if someone needs to talk."

"I'll make sure he's here if I have to bring him myself." George finished his beer, stood and shook hands with Jethro. "Thanks, man. You're a good guy and we're lucky to have you living among us."

"No thanks necessary, George."

CHAPTER 22

SHERIFF LOGAN SPENT A sleepless night preparing the talk he was going to have with Pete Tucker in the morning. He didn't want Pete to know he had met with Dusty and Carrie, but he planned to put the fear of God into him so the vandalism would stop.

He took a final swig of his cold coffee and headed for the front door. "On my way to work, Abs," he hollered up to his wife. "I'll stop in for some afternoon delight if you're up to it," he chuckled.

Abigail stood at the top of the stairs in her bra and panties, hands on her hips, grinning down at her husband. "You still think you got it, don't you, Georgie boy," she laughed.

"Yes, ma'am. I sure do."

"Well, you can get those thoughts right out of your head. I'm meeting Sadie for breakfast. We're going to plan a baby shower for Meredith."

"How about a kiss before I leave then?" he puckered up and opened his arms wide. His heart started beating fast looking at Abs in her lacy underwear. He grinned, thinking it was bad enough she could turn him on with just her smile, and here she was standing half-naked. *Down boy!*

She heaved a giant sigh as she sauntered down the

steps. "Oh, I suppose so, if it'll get you out of the house."

Abigail loved teasing and bantering back and forth with her husband. It was a ritual they'd been doing all of their married life which kept the sparks between them smoldering. After thirty-eight years of marriage, they were still deeply in love. She walked into her husband's open arms and he closed them around her, hugging her tightly and nuzzling her neck.

Abigail frowned. George wasn't usually this frisky or affectionate first thing in the morning. "Everything okay, George?"

"Yeah. I just have a lot on my mind. Guess I needed a hug."

She embraced him tighter and turned her face up to him. "I'll take that kiss now."

George leaned down, placed a tender kiss on her lips, his tongue teasing lightly, and ran his hand over her bottom. "That good enough for ya' or do you want more, 'cause I got more?"

Pulling away, Abigail said, "That'll get you in trouble. Now get on with you. Get to work." She nudged him toward the door. "Call me if you need me. I'll have my cell on."

George grabbed his hat and placed it on his head. He gave his wife a devilish look. "You sure you're busy later?" Glancing at the scowl on his wife's face, he raised his hands, "Never mind." Laughing, he left. Walking toward his vehicle he thought, *I sure do love that woman.*

Abigail stood at the window watching George as he drove out of the driveway. She had a gut instinct something was wrong, but rarely did he talk to her about his business. Whatever it was, she hoped it would blow over soon.

WHEN GEORGE ARRIVED AT the office, he smelled coffee brewing and noticed Sawyer had cleaned up the little kitchenette. *We must have lived like pigs before she joined the force.* He grabbed a mug, filled it with the steaming black liquid and replaced the pot so it could continue its cycle. "Any muffins?" he asked his deputy.

"Not my turn," she kidded.

"Did you bring any muffins, Viv?"

"Not my turn either," she said, clicking away with her knitting needles.

George walked over to an empty desk and plunked down heavily into a chair. "Have either of you seen Pete this morning?"

"Yeah. We got a call that someone hit a deer. He and Ed went to move it out of the way," Vivian told him.

Sawyer had no experience when it came to dead deer in the road and asked, "Will they leave it there on the side of the road?"

"Probably, or give it to the person who called it in, if they want it. If not, Mother Nature or animals will take care of it."

"That's really gross, George." Sawyer wrinkled up her nose as if she smelled something putrid.

"That's the way things are out here. You'll get used to it." Before George picked up the morning newspaper he asked, "How do you like your new place?"

"I love it. Thanks for asking." She stared at him, eyebrow raised.

George began scanning the paper and glanced at her over his spectacles. "What?"

"What's going on?" she asked. "You're not usually this quiet."

"I'm not looking forward to having a talk with Pete this morning. I know it's something I have to do, and I have to do it now. I don't want Jethro to press charges and so far, he's willing to keep what he knows to himself. You got something going on with him?"

"Who?"

"Don't play games with me, Missy. You know damn well who I'm talking about. If I have to spell it out for you I will, G.U.N.N.Y."

"I don't know what you're talking about. We're just friends, and barely that. He's a royal pain in my rump and most times, he's meaner than a snake. If it wasn't for his dog, I wouldn't go near him."

"That why your face is getting all red?"

"Leave it alone, Sheriff." She turned and headed out to the kitchenette. "I need some coffee."

AN HOUR LATER, PETE and Ed returned. George stood up, stretched and tucked in his shirt. "How'd it go out there?" he asked.

"Fine," Ed answered. "Sam Barlow hit the deer when he was on his way to town. Said he couldn't avoid her, she jumped right in front of him. We let him take her. He said he'd take care of dressing her out and would have plenty of meat in the freezer for his family."

"That's good. Sawyer, here, thinks it's gross to leave the poor things on the side of the road."

"Well, that's the way it is around here," Ed parroted what George had said earlier. "You'll get used to it."

"I doubt that," she said, making a face.

"Pete. Why don't you grab a cup of coffee and meet me in my office."

"What's up, Sheriff?" he asked.

"Just something I want to run by you, if you don't mind." He gave Pete a look so that the deputy knew it was an order, not a request. "Five minutes."

"Yup. I'll be right there." Pete Tucker's stomach constricted into a tight knot, and he could feel beads of perspiration forming on his forehead. He quickly wiped them away. He wondered how much George knew and if after the meeting, the sheriff would arrest him.

"Come on in, Pete. Have a seat." George motioned to a chair in front of his desk.

"What's up?" he asked, sitting down on the hard, wooden

seat.

"How've you been?

"Me? I've been fine, fine." Pete took a sip of his coffee.

"I don't think so," George told him. "There's a hardness about you, Pete, something I haven't seen in a long time; you're jumpy, you take off and no one knows where you are. I hate to do this, but I want you to take a urine test…now."

Pete's eyes narrowed, his nostrils flared and his face turned hard. "You gotta' be shitting me, George. I'm not taking a piss test and that's that."

George stood and leaned across his desk, hands splayed. "Don't forget who the sheriff is Pete. You're either going to take the test or I'm going to fire you, right here, right now."

"On what charge?" Pete fidgeted in his seat.

"Don't even make me go there," the sheriff warned. "You gonna' take the test or are you going home?"

Pete sat quiet for several minutes. "I won't pass, George."

"I didn't think so."

"Am I done?" he asked, fingering his badge in an attempt to remove it from his shirt.

"Hold on. I'm prepared to offer you an alternative. If you don't take it, then you're done." The sheriff sat back down and looked intently at Pete, his deputy, his friend, and someone who desperately needed help.

"What's the offer?" Pete knew for sure he wasn't going to like going back into rehab which he figured George would probably suggest.

"You're going to start monthly meetings with Jethro Byrd and the other vets he has working for him. If you need to meet more than once a month, we can arrange it. You will *not* miss a meeting or you'll be canned, not only by me but by the gunny." He glanced at Pete and swore he could see sheer hatred on his face.

"What about if I go back to rehab instead?"

"You don't get to make the rules, Pete. You're going to do as I suggest or that's it."

"I hate that cocky son-of-a-bitch," Pete bellowed. "I can't do it, George. It's never gonna' work."

Pete's outburst shocked the sheriff. "What's he ever done to you? I thought you didn't know him."

"Long story."

"The next meeting is Thursday night at 7 o'clock. Be there." George pushed his chair back and stood up. "I'm putting you on administrative leave with pay until you can show me a clean urine test. That's because we're friends. I need your gun and your shield," he said, holding out his hand.

"Do they know about this?" he pointed to the other room where Ed and Sawyer were working. Pete opened his holster and removed his revolver, then unfastened his shield. He passed them to George.

"Nope. This is between you and me." The sheriff knew he would have to tell Ed, but he didn't want Pete to feel more embarrassed than he already was. He felt a little white lie wouldn't hurt under the circumstances.

CHAPTER 23

A COMMOTION FROM THE alpaca herd woke Sawyer from a deep sleep. Fearing a wild animal might have gotten into the pen, she jumped out of bed, grabbed her gun from the nightstand and ran out to the back porch.

Her heart gave a small lurch at the sight before her…a baby alpaca! Adorable! She didn't even know one of the girls, as she called them, was pregnant. Anxious to get a better look at the new baby, Sawyer slipped her bare feet into an old pair of sneakers that she kept by the door, and made her way down the steps to the fence.

The beige little baby, in the midst of the herd, suckled on its mother while the rest of the females sniffed and made humming sounds. The girls acted like a family of maiden aunts, ready to jump in and babysit if needed.

Sawyer was about to open the gate and go into the pasture when she noticed a lone rider coming through the field. She shielded her eyes against the morning sunlight and watched as Jethro came into sight. *What is he doing here?*

He rode up close to the herd on his pinto, Domino, with Mabel running along beside him. Sawyer's breath caught. Just looking at him made her want him. He looked extra fine this morning in his worn denim jacket, blue plaid shirt, tight jeans, which outlined his muscular legs, and scuffed, brown cowboy boots. His crooked grin was captivating and she stifled a groan.

As Jethro rode closer, he could see Sawyer's copper hair glimmering in the sunlight. His gut contracted at the sight of her and as much as he enjoyed the feelings, it terrified him. He jumped down off his horse and sauntered over to the fence. "You can close your mouth now," he teased.

"Oh," she stamped her foot. "You are such an …."

"Just kidding." He laughed, knowing he had gotten under her skin. "What do you think of the baby girl? She was born yesterday around noontime." He gave Sawyer the once over, gazing at her nipples which had become taut. His lingering eyes on her body reminded Sawyer that she was standing in her pajamas with very little on underneath.

She crossed her arms over her chest and gave him the evil eye. "I'll be right back," she said indignantly as she stomped up the steps and into her house. She felt as if he had undressed her right there in the back yard. It unnerved and excited her, imagining what making love with him would be like.

She dallied with the idea of just throwing a sweatshirt over her PJ's, but thought better of it. Instead, she fully dressed, and secured her hair back from her face with a headband before hurrying outside. She leaned against the fence watching Jethro in the pasture.

He was busy checking the baby, rubbing her back, talking gently. Then he wrapped his arm around her neck and cuddled her. Sawyer swore the little girl lifted her head for a kiss. He had that way with all females, she guessed. Jethro became aware of her watching him and gestured. "Come on in."

"Are you sure? I've been dying to touch them, but didn't know if I'd get attacked."

"That wouldn't happen. Alpacas are gentle and enjoy interaction with their own and with humans. Come over here and pat one. The baby is called a Cria," he added, nuzzling the newborn again.

Sawyer walked slowly to the middle of the herd, still a little wary to be among these large animals. As soon as she stepped forward, they moved closer, curious to check her out. They sniffed her and then let her pet them. She spoke in a soft voice, more to calm herself down than anything else. She was amazed how thick and soft their fleece was. One brown and white female tried to take the headband off her hair, but Jethro gave a little nudge and the alpaca moved away.

"So what do you think?" he asked.

"I fell in love with them the first time I spotted them in the pasture. They have the cutest faces and I love the humming sound they make. One of these days, when I have enough money to buy a little ranch, I'm going to own some alpacas."

Jethro admired her spirit and knew she would accomplish whatever she set out to do. He only hoped her dream of owning a home and a ranch would be with him.

"By the way, what are you doing here anyway?" she asked.

He could lie, or he could tell her the truth. He decided he'd better tell the truth and take his tongue-lashing, which he knew was coming. She was a tiny little thing, but meaner than a badger when she was mad. "Would you believe me if I told you I was just riding by?" He cocked an eyebrow and flashed that bad boy smile which made her knees wobble.

"Ah, that would be a no. What's going on Jethro?" Sawyer knew she wasn't going to like his answer by the way he avoided eye contact with her, but she didn't have a clue what he was going to say.

Jethro cleared his throat, a clear indication he was nervous. "Okay, I own these alpacas, I own all this land, and I own the house you are living in." He took a quick step back in case she wanted to take a swing at him.

"Are you kidding? I suppose everyone in town knows you own half of Stony Creek," she said sarcastically, "but they failed to mention it to me." Anger flared in her eyes as she blinked back tears. Her feelings were hurt and she was mad. She marched over to Jethro and gave him a little push on the shoulder. Her fingers felt like fire when she touched him. "Go home!" she ordered.

He touched her arm and she jerked away as if scalded. "Mac, there was no reason to tell you."

"I asked everyone I knew who owned the house and no one would tell me. Why was that? And quit calling me Mac!"

"I guess they suspected you wouldn't rent the house if you knew I owned it."

"Well, you got that right! I'm giving you a 30-day notice, right now." She pushed her way around him and headed toward the gate.

Jethro grabbed her arm and pulled her toward him. "Mac, don't make a hasty decision. You're not living here free. You're paying rent, you obviously love the place, and look, all these alpacas are here for you to enjoy. I heard you want to get a dog, too. Think about it, please."

The last thing he wanted was for Sawyer to move out. He loved having her close so he could be on hand if she needed him. Not that she'd ever ask for help, but his men kept him apprised of her comings and goings.

"Get your hands off me," she shouted, pulling away from him. "I'll be out of your hair so fast you'll never know I was here." She slammed the gate and trounced off into the house.

Jethro stood there for several minutes wondering what he could do to make her change her mind. Not able to come up with a reasonable answer, he whistled for Domino who had wandered away to graze. She heard his whistle and came galloping to him. Climbing into the saddle, he looked at the house one more time, hoping to catch a glimpse of Sawyer, turned and rode off toward his ranch.

SAWYER STOOD JUST OUT of sight and watched Jethro ride away. She was crying like a baby. She couldn't stay in this house now because of the emotions whirling around inside her whenever he was near. The attraction was too strong and not reciprocated. Oh, she was well aware that he wanted to make love to her, but she doubted he would ever be committed. A hopeless romantic, she wanted more than a roll in the hay. She deserved more.

Hearing a car in the driveway, she wiped her tears away and went to see who it was. *It had better not be Jethro.* Looking out the kitchen window, Sawyer saw Meredith getting out of her truck with something in her hand. She went outside to greet her.

"Hey, Meredith. Welcome."

Meredith waved as she made her way to the house. "Hi. Thought I'd bring you a little housewarming gift," she said, holding up a pretty yellow bag.

"You didn't have to do that, but come on in. I'm glad to have company. Do you have time for a cup of coffee?"

"The babies don't like coffee, but I'll take a cup of tea if you have any, or water."

"Tea it is," Sawyer said, putting the kettle on the stove. "Do you want to look around, or have you already seen the place?"

Meredith frowned. "Why would you say that?" she asked, setting the bag on the table.

"Well, I just found out that Jethro Byrd owns this house, this land, and God knows what else. Seems like it was a big secret and I'm the last to know. I gave him my 30-day notice when he told me."

"Do you think that was wise? Sadie told me you love this place."

"I do love it. That's going to be the hardest part about leaving. I'll probably have to go back to Charlie and Sadie's until I find something else."

The teakettle whistled and Sawyer went to the stove to stop the annoying sound. She opened a canister of tea bags and placed them on the table along with two mismatched cups and saucers. "Sorry about the dishes. They came with the house."

"Hey, a cup is a cup. We don't go in for much formality around these parts. What you see is what you get." She smiled at Sawyer.

"How are you feeling?" Sawyer asked Meredith. "I see a baby bump."

Meredith rubbed her belly and grinned. "I'm feeling great now the morning sickness is over. I thought I was going to die in the beginning."

Sawyer laughed. "How's Dakota holding up?"

"He's been wonderful. He's going to be a great dad to these little ones. He figured he'd never get married much less be a father so he's enjoying it, morning sickness and all."

"Did you say little ones? Twins?"

"Yup, I'm getting it all over with the first time," she beamed.

"Congratulations. I hope I'm that lucky. I'm already thirty-three so my eggs are screaming at me to get with it," she chuckled.

"Hey, I'm thirty-eight, thirty-nine when the babies get here, so never give up hope. Now let's get back to you moving out of this house. Don't you think you're biting off your nose to spite your face?"

"I don't think it was fair that no one told me what I was getting into."

"What are you getting into? You wanted a place of your own, and by the way, this place is adorable, and the rent is affordable. I don't understand the problem."

Confused, Sawyer wondered if she had spoken too soon. Indecision gnawed at her. "What do you think I should do?"

"I think you should cowgirl up, give Jethro a call and tell him you've changed your mind."

Sawyer shook her head. "Oh, I could never do that. He'd love it. He'd laugh me right out of Stony Creek. I can see it now."

"I think you have him all wrong. He's one of the kindest men around and has been a wonderful asset to the town. He's like a ten-year-old boy. If he's teasing you, it's because he likes you. Good thing you don't have braids and an inkwell handy," she snickered.

"Make sure you're calm before calling him though. I'll bet he'll be happy to hear from you and hasn't given your notice a moment's thought. Well, I have to get back to the diner," she said, pushing her chair back and standing up. "Oh, don't you want to open the gift I got for you?"

"Of course. I'm sorry. I was so wrapped up in myself I wasn't thinking about anything else." She picked up the heavy bag and frowned as she untied the ribbon holding the handles together. Peeking inside, she stuck her hand in and removed tissue paper revealing a horseshoe. She gave Meredith a curious look.

"It's for good luck. Hang it over your front door with the ends facing up so the good luck won't fall out and the devil can't get in."

"Seriously?"

"Seriously," Meredith grinned.

Sawyer gave her a big hug. "I can't begin to thank you for stopping by today and for the gift. You're like the big sister I never had. I appreciate your advice. I think I'll have a cold beer to give me courage and then I might give that old marine a call," she giggled.

CHAPTER 24

PETE TUCKER BOUNCED ALONG the dirt road in his pickup, a pine-scented air freshener swinging back and forth from the rear view mirror. The truck shuddered as it hit a rut and he slowed down. The crackle of tires rolling over the ground was giving him a headache. He rubbed his temple with his fingers and shook his head trying to ward off the invading pain.

It was Thursday evening and he was on his way to attend a mandatory meeting with Jethro Byrd along with the other screw-ups that worked for him as ranch hands. This was the last thing he wanted to do, but George threatened to fire him if he didn't show up. Pete would sooner dig ditches or clean outhouses than spend ten minutes having his brain picked by the gunny. He had no idea what to expect, but he was sure he wasn't going to have a good time.

Pete had seen Jethro in town many times since he arrived in Stony Creek four years ago. He had never had an encounter with him while performing his deputy duties, but he had reason to hate the cocky bastard.

When Pete was seventeen, he joined the Marine Corps. The day the bus pulled into boot camp, the recruits met a mean, screaming-in-your-face Drill Instructor, Jethro Byrd. From day one, he humiliated and ridiculed them, calling them worthless maggots, mama's boys, dumb stupid girls, and those were on good days. Their identity and all they knew before joining the military had been stripped down, from their civilian clothes to the hair on their heads.

The DI did his best to break their spirits, transitioning them from civilians to recruits. He seemed to enjoy watching them as they passed out or threw up during the grueling physical training.

Despite the required long runs and marches, Jethro ran alongside his men, leading the pack, spurring them on with cadence songs: *I love working for Uncle Sam, Let's me know just who I am, 1 2 3 4 United States Marine Corps, 1 2 3 4 I love the Marine Corps,* and on it would go, mile after mile. Over the course of thirteen weeks, the new recruits made it or they didn't. If they didn't, they got a second chance. No one wanted that second chance because it was more brutal than ever.

Pete was always getting into trouble for screwing up. He spoke when he shouldn't, didn't make his bunk right, and didn't pass rifle inspection, along with numerous other infractions. The gunny rewarded him with hours of running and sit-ups until he thought his muscles would explode, making his life a pure hell until he got it right. Pete hated Jethro's guts and vowed that one day he'd get even.

He set his plan into action when Dusty Boone vandalized the church and Pete caught him. He used Dusty to do his dirty work. That is, until he told Dusty to burn down Jethro's barn. Stupid little kid must have told someone, because everything changed after that.

George had called him in, said he suspected he was dirty, and ordered Pete to attend these meetings. Pete knew the only reason he still had his job was because of their friendship.

Pete pulled over to the side of the road before turning into Jethro's driveway. He checked his watch. He was early. He pulled an opened pack of Pall Mall's from his shirt pocket, removed a cigarette and lit it. He inhaled a large drag and blew it out. Tendrils of smoke curled around him as he tried to calm his nerves.

JETHRO WATCHED Pete Tucker's truck make its way toward the house. The rest of the men were already there and knew the deputy would be joining them. As soon as Pete pulled up, Jethro went onto the porch and waited for him.

"Pete. Glad to see you could make it," he said, extending his hand.

Pete ignored the welcome. "Yah. Wish I could say the same."

Jethro ignored the rebuff, opened the door and motioned for Pete to go in. "Come on. I'll introduce you to the guys."

"How long does this meeting last?" he asked.

"As long as we need it to. Let's not worry about that now. You don't have to do anything. You can just sit and listen if you want to, or if you have something to say, we'll listen."

They entered the great room. Six men dressed as cowboys stood up while Jethro introduced them to Pete. "This is Joe, Bob, Fred, John, Mike, and Sam, all veterans of Iraq." They greeted him respectfully. Jethro wouldn't have had it any other way.

"We got coffee over there if you want a cup," Fred told Pete.

"No thanks."

"Well, let's get started then," Jethro told the men. "Have a seat everyone." He looked at Pete. "The only rule we have is no drinking or using drugs."

Pete fidgeted and sat on the edge of a big leather armchair. He looked around at the men. The first thing he noticed was that each man had a dog lying beside him. He leaned forward and a black and tan German shepherd sat up and let out a deep, ominous growl. Pete quickly sat back in his chair.

"Hey! No, Frankie! Down," Joe ordered his dog, patting him on his haunches. "Sorry about that," he said to Pete. "Frankie here thinks he has to protect me."

Jethro explained. "All of these dogs are specially trained to help veterans who are facing difficult problems. They're taught to awaken them from night terrors, and can sense when a veteran is about to have a panic attack. The dog will nudge him, which will cause him to refocus. They make the perfect buddy, just like the buddy who had his back when he was in battle.

"I'd probably be dead now if I didn't have Sally," John said, reaching down to pet his yellow Lab. "It might do you some good to have a dog of your own." He looked squarely at Pete.

"I don't much like dogs. They're always getting under foot."

Frankie growled again. "Excuse me." Joe got up, took Frankie's leash, and ordered him to heel. They went out through the kitchen and Pete heard a door slam.

"He's redirecting his dog by giving him a time out. It usually works, too," Bob said. "But we hate to do it."

"Who's got something they want to discuss?" Jethro asked.

"I do," Mike said.

"Go ahead Mike."

Sensing that her master was anxious, Bonnie, Mike's black Catahoula dog, sat up and put her head on his lap. Mike rubbed her head. He proceeded to discuss a recurring dream he was having about the bomb that killed three men in his unit. He felt guilty that he was still alive and didn't die with them. He should have died, since he was on point that day. Mike was suffering from a syndrome commonly referred to as Survivor's Guilt.

The meeting lasted almost two hours before Pete could go home. He knew he would have to go back, but no one could make him spill his guts the way the other men were doing. No way in hell was he going to do that.

CHAPTER 25

SAWYER WAS ABOUT TO leave for work when the phone rang. She looked at her cell and noticed it was the realtor. "Hello."

"Hi Sawyer. It's Nola Cummings. How are you today?"

"I'm fine, thanks. And you?"

"Fine here. The reason I'm calling is that Jethro told me you gave him a 30-day notice and I have someone interested in the house."

Sawyer felt a moment of panic. Why didn't she call Jethro to let him know she had changed her mind? Her silly pride had gotten in the way, and now she might lose the place she had come to love. *I would have called him eventually,* she thought.

"I've had a change of heart," she told Nola. "I was angry when I gave him the notice, but after thinking it over, I've decided to stay, if he'll let me."

"Are you sure?" Nola asked.

"Positive."

"Okay then. I'll get back to Jethro and the clients who wanted the house."

"Nola? How did anyone know this house might be for rent?"

"I told you before; word travels fast in a small town. Gotta' scoot. Take care, Sawyer," Nola disconnected the call.

Sawyer's anger was immediate. *How dare he tell*

everyone I was going to move when it was his fault I gave him the notice in the first place. If he hadn't lied, I wouldn't have gotten so mad at him. I thought he wanted me to stay, he said so, but I guess I was wrong. Sawyer started to dial Jethro's number when she noticed the time. She was going to give him a piece of her mind, but she was late for work. It could wait.

TWENTY MINUTES LATER, SAWYER parked her cruiser behind the station. When she entered the office, George was leaning back in his chair reading the paper, Ed was doing a crossword puzzle, and Pete was noticeably absent.

"Morning everyone. Sorry I'm late."

"Heard you were moving," George said, not looking up and turning a page of the paper.

"Oh for God's sake. Word gets around this town quicker than a high school rumor. I am not moving!"

"Glad to hear it. Fresh pot of coffee out back."

"How's Pete doing?" she asked.

"He went to his first meeting. He wasn't happy about it, but Jethro said he showed up and stayed until it was over."

Ed looked up from his crossword. He put his pencil behind his ear, uncomfortable about what he was going to disclose. He and Pete had been friends since they were kids and he felt guilty ratting on him. However, he felt George should know what was going on under the current circumstances. "Pete's drinking again, and I suspect he's smoking pot, too," he blurted out.

George put his paper down and sat upright. "How do you know this?"

"I was at the Smokin' Barrel the other night and Pete walked in. I was sitting in the back, and he didn't see me. He ordered three shots in a row and a beer, and then left."

George shook his head. "Guess I'll take a ride out to his place this morning and make an impromptu visit. What you just told me will stay among us." He pushed back his chair and got up to leave. “Ed, you stay here and man the phones. Vivian is volunteering at the nursing home this morning. Sawyer, make yourself visible in town and then take a ride on the back roads to see what’s going on, if anything.”

There were times when George was all business, and his deputies addressed him accordingly. “Yes, sir,” she answered. She put on her hat and headed for the door.

GEORGE WASN’T LOOKING FORWARD to an encounter with Pete, but if what Ed told him was true, he needed to find out. Pete was a loose cannon these days, and the sheriff was concerned for Maddy and their kids.

It was all quiet when he pulled up in front of Pete’s house on Culpepper Road. Maybe too quiet. No dogs running up to greet him, no lights on in the house, just sort of eerie. The hair on the back of his neck stood up, and his skin prickled. He didn’t have a good feeling at all.

George unsnapped his holster before he exited the vehicle. He started toward the house in slow, cautious movements, alert for any sounds coming from the inside or outside. There were none. The lump in George’s throat felt big as an apple. His mouth was dry and he had a hard time swallowing. He knew he should call for backup, but this was Pete for heaven’s sake, his friend. Pete would never hurt him.

The sheriff slowly made his way to the front door. He rapped three times, stepped back to increase his own personal space, and waited. When no one answered, he knocked again and called out. “Pete, Maddy, you in there?” He was trying to think ahead as to what might happen next.

Again, no answer. George was still unnerved, but figured maybe he was making too much out of nothing. He turned to leave when he heard the front door creak open. His hand went to his holster as he turned around.

Maddy was standing in the doorway, Pete to one side of her, several days’ stubble on his face. “There you two are. I was beginning to wonder if you'd gone to town and I missed you," George said, trying to keep his voice cheery. "Thought I'd stop in and see how you're doing."

"We were taking a nap," Maddy said.

"Hmmm. Strange time of day to be taking a nap I'd say. Mind if I come in?" Before either of them could answer, George pushed past Maddy and let himself into the house.

"Pete, old buddy," George said, slapping him on his shoulder. "How's things going?" He could smell alcohol on Pete's breath, and noticed his eyes were glassy.

Maddy's shoulders and the forced smile on her face relaxed when George entered the house. He noticed how she was nervously wringing her hands and her eyes were darting back and forth to Pete. The sheriff had seen enough spousal abuse in his career to recognize the signs of a frightened woman. He also saw what looked like a bruise on the side of her face.

"Maddy. Would you mind fixing me a cup of coffee?"

"Sure, Sheriff."

"Pete. Can we talk?" George started for the living room. "Let's go in here and have a seat."

"I'm not in the mood for an interrogation, if that's what you plan to do," Pete responded.

"I didn't plan on interrogating you, but since you put it that way, it does smell like you've been drinking. Am I right?"

"I had a couple of beers this morning," Pete admitted. "But only this one time. Had a headache that wouldn't go away and thought the beer might help."

George knew Pete was lying, but decided not to push the issue until he could figure what the dynamic was in the household. "Are the headaches worse, Pete?"

"I get them more often now and it takes a long time before they go away."

"What about your nightmares?"

"Still get those, too."

"How did you feel at the meeting the other night? Do you think you're going to get something out of it?"

"Hell no. Just a bunch of sniveling misfits, sharing war story nightmares, wanting sympathy. They all had dogs and wanted me to get one. I told them no. I hate dogs."

Ignoring his remark, George asked, "Where are your dogs, anyway? They usually come running to greet me."

"I got rid of 'em. Too damn noisy for their own good. Gave me headaches."

"I'll bet the kids were sad and upset to see them go."

"They'll get over it. It is what it is."

Maddy brought the mugs into the living room and set them on the coffee table. Her hands were trembling, and some of the hot liquid sloshed out.

Pete looked at her with contempt. "Can't you ever do anything right?" he snarled.

"Sorry," she murmured, wiping up the spill with her apron.

George saw the hurt in her eyes. "Hey, Pete, it was an accident. I imagine the coffee was hot."

"Whatever. You can leave us alone now, Maddy."

Maddy turned, but not before shooting a pleading look at George.

"Pete. We've been friends a long time, and I'm very concerned about you. No way can you come back to work if you're drinking. We need to figure out a way to get rid of those headaches. They're making you mean, and you're doing things you'd never do if you were feeling good."

"What do you mean by that?' Pete took a sip of his coffee, wishing it were a beer.

"I've never heard you say a mean word to your wife until today. She's a nervous wreck. I'm going to assume from the bruise on her face perhaps you've been hitting her. If that's the case, it can't happen again."

"You really should mind your own damn business, George. No man is going to tell me how to run my household."

"I'm Sheriff of this county, and I'm not going to stand by and watch a man abuse his wife. It's my job, and you know it. You used to feel the same way."

"I think it's time you left now. This little "howdy" session is over." Pete stood up, walked to the door and held it open. "Come by another time when you can't stay so long."

George walked to the door and looked Pete in the eye. "Get your shit together, Pete, or you're not going to like the consequences." As the sheriff walked down the front steps, he heard the door slam behind him.

George was worried. *We got big trouble here.*

SAWYER WAS TRAVELLING DOWN Culpepper Road, taking her time and enjoying the scenery, when she noticed a dark red stain on the gravel. She pulled over to inspect it and realized it was blood leading to a pasture across the road. Not knowing what she might find, she took a rifle from the rack in the back of the cruiser and walked toward the field. She had only gone a few feet when she heard whimpering. A moment later, a small black and tan puppy came out of the grass, wagging his tail, but in obvious pain.

Sawyer sat down and put her hand out to the little dog. "Come here, sweetie," she coaxed in a soft voice. The pup bowed his head and crouched down on its belly, crawling toward her in a submissive manner. She coaxed the pup some more, and it turned over on its back. It was then she noticed it was a boy.

Her heart broke. She didn't think a car had hit him. It looked as if someone had beaten him. His small head was bloody, one eye swollen shut, and it appeared one of his legs was broken. He couldn't have been more than four or five months old. *Who would do such a thing to a defenseless little animal? God help the person if I ever find out.*

Sawyer petted the puppy and talked gently to him.

"It's okay, boy. Everything is going to be fine." She didn't know where the nearest vet was, but she did know that one of the men who lived at Jethro's had some vet experience. She pulled out her cell and dialed his number.

"Byrd here."

"Jethro, this is Sawyer. I'm out on Culpepper and found a badly injured puppy. It looks like someone beat him. Can I bring the pup out there? He needs treatment immediately or I'm afraid he's not going to make it."

"You stay put. Mike and I will be right out. He'll assess the pup's injuries before we try to move him."

"Thanks, but please hurry."

CHAPTER 26

IMPATIENLY, SAWYER WAITED FOR Jethro. She couldn't understand what was taking him so long. She worried whether the injured pup would make it.

Hearing a vehicle approaching, she stood up. *Finally.*

The truck came to a halt. Jethro and Mike climbed out and rushed to her.

"Thanks for coming. Here he is," she gestured to the puppy lying beside her.

Mike stooped down and gave him a quick examination. "He's pretty beat up," he said as he scooped the little dog up in his arms, "but I'll take good care of him."

Jethro fumed. "Mac, I hope you find the person who did this. When you do, give me two minutes with the bastard and I'll teach him a lesson he won't forget."

Sawyer despised the person responsible for this and she could envision Jethro doing what he said. She admired his concern and sense of justice, but he'd have to stand in line when it came to punishing the person who harmed the puppy.

"Gunny. We need to get going," Mike said, already walking toward the truck.

Jethro gave Sawyer a longing glance. "We'll take good care of him." He ran to the truck.

"Thanks again," she hollered. "I'll check with you later to see how he's doing." Sawyer wasn't sure he heard her as she watched him drive away.

"COME HERE, LITTLE GIRL," Sawyer coaxed the baby alpaca whom she had named Ally. Each morning before work, she would gaze over the fence, watching the herd graze and play. The scene was calming and captivating, starting her day off just right.

Sawyer unlatched the gate and went into the pasture. Once she learned how gentle the animals were, she had begun interacting with them. She had named each of them based on their unique personality.

Millie, a sweet, medium fawn color, was Ally's mother. Sawyer loved to hear Millie cluck to her baby, just as human mothers do.

Gracie, a beautiful, pregnant, rose gray, seemed to be the most curious of the eight females in the herd. Usually she was the first one at the fence checking out what was happening. Sawyer was excited there was going to be a new addition. She hoped to be around for the birth. A boy would be nice to add to the family.

She adored all of them, but especially loved the little Cria she named Ally. One of these days, she hoped she'd have enough money to buy her. Maybe she could make a deal with Jethro.

Ally ambled over to Sawyer and nudged her hand, looking for her daily treat of cut up carrot slices. Sawyer pulled a plastic baggy out of her jeans pocket, catching the attention of the other alpacas. Before she knew it, they were all standing around her, excited and waiting for their treat. She fed and petted each girl before heading for the gate with Ally following behind her.

Immediately, Millie started clucking, making a high-pitched hum as soon as Ally was out of her sight. The small Cria turned and ran back to her mother.

SAWYER HAD THE DAY off. After finishing her morning coffee and a strawberry yogurt, she took a long, hot shower. After toweling off, she added a splash of Jean Nate′ to her body. Brushing the tangles from her long, copper tresses, she gave a slow, back and forth toss of her hair, before letting it air dry while she dressed.

She opened the closet door and stood for several minutes trying to decide what to wear. It should be a no-brainer: shirt, jeans, and boots, but she wanted to look especially attractive today. She planned to visit the injured puppy to see how he was coming along, but in reality, she was hoping to run into Jethro.

She deliberately hadn't called to let him know she was coming by. Sawyer didn't want to admit that possibly seeing him was why she was feeling so giddy. Jethro Byrd with his amazing blue eyes, bad boy smile and flippant ways drove her crazy, and she had to confess he turned her on as no other man had ever done.

Sawyer pulled a turquoise-checked long-sleeved shirt from a hanger and slipped it on, admiring the lovely antique bronze snaps which accentuated it. She slid her legs into a pair of low-rise boot cut jeans, and added a brown leather belt with a brass buckle. She walked over to the bed and sat down to pull on her boots, wondering if they were ever going to stretch enough to be comfortable.

Never one for much makeup, a dab of blush, a touch of lip gloss and she was ready to go. She grabbed her straw raffia cowgirl hat with matching turquoise bling around the band, took one last look in the mirror and headed out the door.

Sawyer jumped into the cruiser, wishing she knew how to ride a horse so she could make her way through the pasture to Jethro's ranch. She needed to put that on her "to do" list if she planned to live in Montana for the rest of her life.

JETHRO SAT ON THE porch steps drinking coffee, the warm morning sun seeping into his skin. He'd lived on this ranch for four years, and the scene before him was as picturesque now as it was when he first moved here. Mabel lounged close by in a pool of sunlight.

The majestic Tobacco Root Mountains loomed upward before him, their peaks still heavily covered with snow, and puffy white clouds floated aimlessly by. A horse neighed in the distance. He watched a family of white-tailed deer having an early morning breakfast at the base of the tree line. Chatty magpies demanded his attention, as they swayed on the telephone line.

Jethro's life was almost perfect. He'd moved to a small cowboy town where the townsfolk made him feel welcome, he owned a spread of land most people envied, and his friends were many. Why then was he so lonely? His days were long and his nights longer. He kept busy, but there was a void.

The first year after Angie's death, grief took over his whole being. His heart felt like it was physically breaking. Nothing would take away the pain that was eating him up inside, not booze, not friends, and not the Marine Corps. Everything that ever mattered to him was no longer viable for his existence. He needed to get away. Then came the day when he forced himself back into the world of the living and moved to Montana. It had been a good choice.

Mabel lifted her head, ears perked, and jumped up looking toward the driveway. She barked, ran around in circles, and bounded down the steps when she recognized the vehicle.

Sawyer brought the cruiser to a stop and turned off the ignition. She stepped out and smiled at Mabel. "Hey girl. How you doing?" she asked, bending over to rub the dog's ears, giving her a pat on the back.

Jethro stood up and took another sip of his now cold coffee. The sight of her made his loins tighten and his pulse began racing. She had such a great butt. He wondered if she knew it. “You here on business?” he asked, as she started toward the steps.

“Nope. I was hoping to see the puppy. How’s he doing?” This man did things to her without the slightest touch. Standing there in tight jeans and a black t-shirt, tufts of curly dark hair peeking out of the neckline made her go all sappy inside.

Jethro was tired of playing games with her; he liked her and he wanted her to know how much he cared. Their bantering had become the way they communicated, but he needed her to understand the real him, the good and the bad.

“You want to come inside for coffee? Then we’ll go up to the barn?”

“The barn! You’re keeping that poor little puppy in the barn?” she shouted. “I just don’t get you, Jethro.”

“Don’t be getting all hot and bothered now,” he said, a half-smirk on his face. “He only stays in the barn during the day so he can get some exercise. Mike is with him all the time.”

“Oh.” She felt like an ass for jumping to conclusions. “Sorry I yelled. Has anyone called to claim him? We put flyers up in town.”

“Nope. No one is going to fess up to that kind of abuse.”

“If he’s not claimed in two weeks, I want him. I’ll pay for his medical expenses and all you and Mike have done to get him well.”

“You don’t have enough money to do that,” he said.

His remark irritated her and she couldn’t let it go. “You have no idea how much money I have.”

Jethro shrugged. “Do you want that coffee now?” He turned the doorknob and started inside.

Sawyer wanted to spend time with him today, but things weren’t starting out very well. The good angel on her right shoulder told her it was dangerous to go inside, but the bad angel on her other shoulder whispered, “Don’t be a chicken." Oh, what the hell. She followed him into the house.

"Something wrong?" he asked her.

"No, why?"

"Your mouth is hanging open again." Laughter rumbled out of him.

"Every time I see this place it amazes me." She gazed around at the open beams, large stone fireplace, leather furniture, and massive great room. "Did you build this yourself?"

"I had some help, but it's my design. Want to take a look around?"

"I'd love to," she said and followed him into the kitchen. Mabel trailed behind her.

Stainless steel and granite shone from every corner of the room, and a large window overlooked the mountains. The only thing missing was Emeril Lagasse. "I'm impressed," she said.

She followed him down a hallway, while a fresh pot of coffee was brewing. He opened a door, which led into a large master suite. Sawyer's eyes opened wide, but at least her mouth stayed closed. Before her was an enormous four-poster bed in the center of the room and a fireplace tucked into a wall of stone. As she continued to look, the bed seemed to grow larger and the room smaller. She swallowed loudly.

"Pretty neat, huh? I had this made from timber right on the property. Want to try it out?" he laughed.

She blushed. "Get out of here," she answered, poking him in the chest with her finger, pushing him back into the hall. "Keep going," she ordered, her heart fluttering and her girl parts dancing a tango.

"Well, if you're going to be that way about it, follow me."

Sawyer detected a smirk on his face, as he led her out to an enclosed area of the porch. *Holy, Hannah*, as her grandmother used to say. "You've thought of everything haven't you," she said, looking at the largest hot tub she had ever seen. She would swear it could hold an army or at least a small Cub Scout troop.

Jethro chuckled at her response. "Have you ever been in a hot tub?"

She shook her head. "It's on my bucket list, but I've never gotten around to it," she quipped.

His voice softened, "It's a great way to unwind after a busy day. Seems to me you're always stressed." He moved behind Sawyer and gently put his arms around her waist, pulling her close to him. He hoped she wouldn't push him away. She didn't; instead, she rested her head against his chest. "You should try it sometime," he murmured in her ear. "The warm water and bubbling jets would make you feel untroubled and tranquil." His tone was soothing, like a snake charmer seducing a cobra with his music.

Jethro slowly turned her around to face him. "I don't want to play games anymore, Mac. I never thought I'd say these words again, but I love you. I've loved you from the first time I saw you." He grinned. "All five foot of you walking up to my door on a mission from George. He sure set you up. I'm sorry for not making it easier on you that day, but you had me the minute you stepped out of the cruiser."

Sawyer felt herself soften from the inside out. She stared into his eyes, not quite trusting what he had just told her. She wanted to believe him, but she would just die if he wasn't telling her the truth. She placed both hands on the sides of his face. "Are you sure, Gunny?"

Tears welled up in his eyes, his heart about to burst wide open from fear. "Yup."

His answer made Sawyer respond instinctively. She showered his face with kisses and hugged him with all her might. Taking a step back, she stared into his eyes, which twinkled with something that looked like relief.

"The first time I saw you in the diner, all mean and snarly, I was hooked, but I fought it." She wrapped her arms around his neck again. "I love you, too, Jethro. I've been waiting for you my whole life."

He pulled her face to his and placed his lips on hers, kissing her deeply. He picked her up in his arms, and kissed the hollow of her throat as he headed for the bedroom. Clinging to him for dear life, she pulled his face to hers again and he obliged her with a powerful kiss.

Easing his embrace, Jethro smiled. This was the first time he'd kissed a woman and she growled. His loins tightened.

He stopped at the bedroom door and looked at her, love in his eyes. "We don't have to do this now if you're not ready."

She smiled up at him. The distinctive tingle in her belly let her know she was. "I want you, Gunny."

He leaned in and his mouth settled on hers for one glorious minute before continuing into the room.

It was then that Jethro noticed his dog sprawled on the bed. "Damn! Mabel. Get down!"

CHAPTER 27

MABEL RELUCTANTLY SLID OFF the bed while Jethro stood waiting with Sawyer in his arms. If dogs were capable of giving dirty looks, then Mabel was shooting daggers into him. She took slow, tiny steps to the doorway, ears back, and turned to look one more time with hopes her master had changed his mind.

"Go on, girl," he told her.

Mabel dragged herself out of the room, but lay down just outside. Jethro closed the door with his foot.

He smiled at Sawyer. "I think she's a little jealous. We can make it up to her later, but for now, you are the woman in my life." He walked to the bed and gently placed her on top of the comforter.

He lay down beside her, not wanting to rush the moment. Resting on one elbow, he traced her face with his finger. "You're really beautiful, you know." He drew her hand to his lips and pressed a soft kiss into her palm.

Sawyer felt her cheeks flush. She wanted him as she had never wanted a man before. Her girl parts were dancing the Macarena at this point and her mouth was dry. She didn't think she could speak if her life depended on it. She pulled him toward her with a 'take me now' look.

Jethro got the message. He groaned and covered her mouth with his, feeling her tongue slide against his own. He made a low sound and deepened the kiss. His strong, capable hand moved under her shirt, and he heard a soft moan when he cupped her breast.

Sawyer coiled her arms around his neck and returned his kisses with intensity. She could feel his arousal as his body pressed her deeper into the bed. The smell of aftershave and soap, along with his touch, was all the turn on she needed.

His voice was low and sexy as he asked, “Okay?”

“Okay,” she answered breathlessly.

They hastily undressed. Jethro poised himself over her and looked longingly into her eyes. She gazed back at him, running her hands down his hard belly. She closed her hand around his erection, leading him to where they were ready to go, linking bodies, linking hearts.

THEY LAY IN BED, facing each other, basking in the afterglow of their lovemaking. Jethro pressed his mouth to the hollow of her throat and pulled her closer. “I never thought I’d be this happy again,” he said, his voice husky with emotion.

She responded with a grin. “I’m glad. Maybe now you won’t be such a grump every time I see you.”

He raised up and looked at her. “So that’s why you dragged me, kicking and screaming, into the bedroom. I admire your tenacity my dear.”

His slow, sexy smile made Sawyer’s toes curl. She ran her hands up his belly and over his chest before pulling him toward her for another kiss. She couldn’t seem to get enough of him. He licked and nibbled her mouth, and she felt him getting excited again. The Macarena girls were dancing their brains out….Eeeh, Macarena!

TOTALLY SPENT AND HUNGRY, Jethro got up at the urging of one pissed off Border collie scratching the hell out of the bedroom door. "Okay, girl. I'm all yours." He walked to the door and opened it.

Mabel gave him a disgusted look, but couldn't stay mad at her master for more than a few minutes. She was needy and he knew it.

Jethro knelt on one knee and wrapped his arms around the little collie, much as he had done with Sawyer a while ago. He petted and hugged her, calling her endearing names in a soft, soothing voice. Mabel threw a look at Sawyer as if to say, "You might have had him for a little while, but he's all mine now."

Sawyer sat on the edge of the bed, a sheet covering her naked body, amused at the scene before her. He was as loving with Mabel as he had been with her. "Do you think she's ever going to forgive me?"

Jethro gave her a lusty look, shook his head and decided against another go round. He didn't want her to think making love was all he wanted from her, and he didn't want his dog to get upset again. "You're probably going to have to do some hard sucking up, but she'll come around. I gotta' let her out. Why don't you get dressed and meet me in the kitchen. We'll have some breakfast."

"So you're done with me?" she joked.

"Yup." He flashed her a teasing smile. "For now."

THE GUYS IN THE BUNK house couldn't believe the change in their boss. For the past three weeks he was a different man, smiling, congenial and in good humor most of the time. They also noticed he was gone most evenings, not coming home until late, if at all.

One evening as they sat around the potbellied stove playing cribbage, Mike said, "He must have gotten laid. I can't imagine anything else that would make him grin all the time. I wonder if he knows how stupid he looks."

The other men burst out laughing. "I think you've got one helluva case of pussy envy, Mike," Joe teased.

"So the rest of you couldn't use a roll in the hay?" Mike hesitated, "It's like, been a while you know."

"That's why we're here," Bob spoke up. "No booze, no drugs, no smokes, and no sex. That pretty much takes care of all our addictions."

They all nodded.

Bob continued, "We've been here quite a while now, most of us anyway. I've been here for over two years. I probably have my shit together, but to be honest, I'm afraid to leave. Without the gunny's encouragement, I'm scared I wouldn't make it back into the real world."

"We all have to leave sometime," Sam said. "Mike, you have a wife who's been waiting for you, and a promising career as a veterinarian. Bob, your circumstances are different. Your wife left, but not until you started abusing her. You do have kids, though, and it's never too late to make amends with them."

Fred piped up. "I've been thinking about something for a while. I'm going to ask Gunny for a furlough for two weeks. Booze is my downfall, but I haven't had a drink in eighteen months. I need to see if I can leave the ranch and stay sober."

"Hey man, I'm sure you can," John said, clapping him on the back. "You're one of the strongest guys here. Your dog, Misty, will be with you. She'll keep you in check."

"You're right. What scares me the most is not being able to sit with you guys and talk things over when I'm having a tough day." Fred brushed a tear away. "You men have become my brothers and I appreciate how we help each other, especially through the hard times."

John said, "One thing for sure, Fred, no matter where you are, we'll always be here for you. We're only a telephone call away."

A FEW EVENINGS LATER, Jethro pulled into Sawyer's drive. He knew she was waiting for him and his heart quickened. He had a surprise for her tonight. He opened the truck door and reached inside for the small ball of fur. The pup was ready for his forever home.

Sawyer stood in her open doorway. When she realized what he was carrying in his arms, she ran down the steps to meet him. "Is this who I think it is?"

He grinned. "Sure is. He's all better and waiting for his new momma."

Her eyes filled with tears as he transferred the bundle of energy from his arms to hers. A small tongue licked her face and her heart melted. "Welcome home, Cooper."

CHAPTER 28

BY MID-JUNE, SUMMER HAD arrived in Stony Creek. Spring had been brief except for a few rainy weeks, and then it slid right into summer. The early morning air was usually crisp and cool, but by noontime the temperature was scorching. *Not as sweltering as Florida*, Sawyer thought, *but hot enough.*

Stony Creek was gearing up for Fourth of July festivities, the rodeo and the picnic at the state park. Sawyer had never been to a rodeo and was looking forward to it. She had to work, but it wouldn't prevent her from watching, especially since Jethro and a couple of couple of the guys from the ranch were going to be pick-up men. She remembered the day he told her about his job at the rodeo.

"Mike, John and I are going to be pick-up men," he said to her.

She raised an eyebrow and gave him a dubious look. "Pick-up men?"

"Don't get all bent out of shape," he laughed. "A pick-up man is the one who keeps the riders safe. Two things can happen when the chute gate opens. The rider either makes the eight-second whistle or he gets bucked off."

He paused and gave her time to ask a question. When she didn't, he continued. "Either way, the pick-up men and their horses have to respond with lightning speed. When the cowboy makes the horn and scores an official ride, he quits spurring and hangs on for a rough ride. His horse usually quits bucking and heads straight for the fence."

He smiled when he said, "That's when we earn our money. Our job is to get to the cowboy as fast as possible and let him grab onto our arm, shoulder or the back of our saddle. Then, if all goes well, we'll set him down gently and disappear like ghosts into the background again."

"I can't wait to see you in action," she grinned.

"You've already seen me in action, little lady," he said, pulling her into him for a quick kiss.

Sawyer blushed, remembering how wonderful it had been making love with Jethro.

"See, I've got you thinking. You're going to be all over me when you see me dressed in my rodeo gear." He grinned and she swatted him on the arm.

"Is there any possibility you can get hurt?"

"There's always the chance, but we're careful. The ultimate challenge is during the bull riding. Bulls don't usually go quietly out of the arena. The barrel men and pick-up men distract the bull so the rider can get to safety once he's dumped off. We try to haze the bull out of the arena before he can cause much trouble. Mabel usually comes into the arena with me. She works the bull, nipping at his heels and herds him toward the gate."

"How does she keep from getting kicked?"

"It's her job. She knows how to avoid those bucking hooves, and rarely is a border collie injured. Mabel loves her job and the crowd loves to see her in action."

"It all sounds so exciting. I can't wait to experience it."

LIVING IN A SMALL community like Stony Creek was far better than Sawyer could have ever imagined. The townspeople welcomed her with open arms. Sadie and Meredith nurtured and befriended her. On top of that, she had fallen in love with one of the best guys on earth, she was sure of it. And, she had her own dog.

Slowly she was making new friends. Abigail Logan, the sheriff's wife, had invited her to play bingo one night. Another first for Sawyer. She had accepted Abby's invitation and had a wonderful evening. She even won the jackpot of $20, which she promptly donated back to the hall.

Sawyer hoped to get to know Carrie Boone and Maddy Tucker better as they were close to her age. She needed some girlfriends. However, under the circumstances, being a deputy and with Pete acting out, Sawyer believed that friendships with these two women might have to wait.

As Sawyer made her way down Main Street, the aroma from the Smokin' Barrel Café caused her stomach to rumble. It was nearly two o'clock. She hadn't eaten since breakfast and realized she was hungry. She opened the door and went in.

"Hey, Deputy," Willa Mae greeted her. "Haven't seen you in a while. Have a seat."

Elliott was sitting by himself, texting on his phone. "I think I'll sit over there with Doc. I'll have some coffee and a grilled cheese sandwich, please."

"Coming right up."

Sawyer walked over to Elliott's table. "Howdy, Doc. Mind if I sit with you?"

He didn't look up and continued to text. "Not at all. How've you been?"

Sawyer detected a coolness in Elliott she hadn't experienced before. If she had to guess, it was because she hadn't accepted his proposal of a dinner date. She should probably confront the issue. But, did she really want to go there?

"I've been fine. You?"

"Jim Dandy, here," he answered with a twinge of sarcasm. He still didn't look at her.

"Elliott, are you mad at me?" she asked, unwrapping her napkin-covered utensils.

He looked at her. "Should I be?"

"Honestly, I don't think so. But, instead of beating around the bush, let's talk about it."

He leaned forward, forearms on the table. "I really liked you, Sawyer," he told her. "You were the first woman I had eyes for ever since my wife left me. Did you not want to date me because I have the twins?"

"Oh goodness, no. Don't ever think that. The boys had nothing to do with it. I think they're wonderful and I think you are, too." She sat back in her chair when Willa brought her coffee and placed it on the table.

"I hear you're dating Jethro Byrd. Is it true?"

"It is." She smiled. "He's a good guy and makes me happy."

Elliott could tell by the look on her face she had it bad for the gunny. He knew that Jethro was an upstanding man, but it didn't keep him from feeling just a tad jealous. "Well, I guess if he makes you happy, I should be glad for you. However, I feel a bit slighted, I want you to know that, but it is what it is. I'm just sorry I never had a chance."

"When the right person comes along, it'll happen." She patted his hand. "You won't have to look for it. Wait and see."

Willa brought Sawyer's sandwich. "Can I get you anything to eat, Doc?" she asked.

"How about a piece of humble pie?" he said sheepishly.

AFTER LUNCH, SAWYER CONTINUED her rounds of the stores on Main Street. She was about to enter Sadie's vintage store when her pager went off.

"Deputy Mackenzie," she answered.

It was the dispatcher, Vivian Brown. "Deputy. I just got a 911 call from Maddy Tucker. She says Pete is on a rampage and you should hurry. She sounded scared out of her wits."

"I'll get right out there. Let Ed know and the sheriff, too, in case I need some back up."

Sawyer's adrenalin was pumping as she ran to her cruiser. She jumped inside. Her stomach tightened not knowing what she was going to encounter when she got to Pete's house. She turned on the lights and siren and sped out of town, signaling to Maddy that help was on the way.

PETE HEARD THE SIRENS and looked menacingly at his wife. He grabbed her arm and yanked her toward him. "Did you call the fucking sheriff on me?"

Maddy cringed, turned her face away from him, but didn't answer.

"I asked you a question, woman," he yelled, grabbing her jaw and twisting her around to look at him.

"Pete, you're hurting me. Stop," she cried.

"Pete, you're hurting me," he mimicked. "I'm going to do more than hurt you if you ever call the sheriff on me again. You hear me!"

Maddy nodded and struggled to get away from her husband's grasp. He held onto her arm tighter, while he took a swig of beer with his other hand. Why was everyone against him? Even his wife. It would be his kids next. He already killed the damn dogs that had turned on him. All except for that runt who got away.

The sound of the siren was getting closer. Pete's anxiety and paranoia were increasing, and his head was beginning to pound. Damn headaches were killing him.

Sawyer pulled into the driveway. "Vivian, I'm at the Tucker's."

"10-4. Ed is on his way. He wants you to wait for him."

Just then, Sawyer heard Maddy scream. She raced from the cruiser, across the yard and up the front steps to the house. She banged on the door. "Pete, open up."

"Get the hell out of here. This is private property and

you're not invited."

"Pete, come outside and let's talk. Bring Maddy out, too."

Sawyer knew she was in a sticky situation. She had to choose her words carefully so as not to set Pete off. "Pete. Will you let Maddy come with me until you're feeling better? You can stay right here. Just let me take her to go pick up the kids from school. Maybe you'll be feeling better by the time we get back. You don't want them getting off the bus, seeing my cruiser here and scaring them."

"She ain't going nowhere. The kids are used to seeing a cruiser in the yard. I'm a deputy. Remember? Or did you forget, since you seem to have taken over my job."

"I didn't take your job, Pete. We're all waiting for you to be well so you can come back to work. We're shorthanded as hell and need you."

"That's a crock of shit and you know it," he snarled. "What'd you do? Call in the troops?" he asked, seeing another cruiser pull in the yard.

Sawyer didn't answer. She was trying to gather her thoughts to decide what they needed to do. She walked over to Ed. "He's in a foul mood, but hasn't threatened. I think he's drunk. I asked him to let Maddy go, but he refused."

"Let me see if I can reason with him. We go way back since we were kids and have worked together for ten years."

Ed walked up onto the porch. He knocked lightly on the door. "Pete. It's me, Ed. Will you let me in?" Getting no response he asked, "Will you come out then?" Still nothing. "Your choice, pal, but we're going to talk, one way or the other."

After a few minutes, the door opened and Pete stepped outside. "Don't worry," he slurred. "I ain't got no gun on me." He pulled out his pocket linings and held his hands in front of him. "See." From his rumpled clothes and unshaven face, Pete looked like he hadn't slept in days. He reeked of alcohol, staggered, and nearly fell off the porch. Ed caught him. “Hang on, old buddy. What’s going on here anyway? Let’s sit down and talk.” Ed helped Pete sit and sat down beside him.

Sawyer stood to one side, her holster unclasped. She was ready to do whatever she needed to do, but prayed it wouldn’t come to that.

“Tell that little bitch to go sit in her vehicle,” Pete demanded.

“You know I can’t do that, Pete. She’s my back up. You remember how that works, pal. We worked many years together and always had each other’s back. I still have your back.” He put his hand on Pete’s shoulder and squeezed.

Pete wrapped both hands around his head. “My fucking head hurts so bad. The pain won’t go away so I drink. I can’t think straight. I know I’ve messed up big time.”

“You need to see a doctor right away. Let me take you over to Fort Harrison and we’ll get you some help. If I can arrange it, will you go?”

“Yah. I need something for the pain. Pot and booze just ain’t cutting it anymore.”

“First though, you have to let Maddy go with Sawyer. Will you do that?”

“I’m afraid if I let her out of my sight, I’ll lose her forever. I can’t do that.”

“How about if we ask her?”

“Yah?” he looked at Ed with bloodshot eyes. “Okay.”

Ed stood up. “Stay right here.” He went to the door, opened it, and motioned for Maddy to come outside. Poor woman. She was a bedraggled mess. Black and blue marks covered her arms and there was a bruise on the side of her face. Ed led her to where Pete was sitting. Maddy was shaking and tears ran down her cheeks.

“Pete. Tell Maddy what you just told me.”

Pete looked up at his wife and started crying. Snot ran out of his nose and he wiped it away with the sleeve of his shirt. “Ed wants me to go to the VA Medical Center, but I’m afraid if I go you won't be here when I get back. I love you, Maddy. I couldn't bear to lose you."

With all the compassion she could muster, Maddy knelt down next to her husband. "Pete Tucker, you know how much I love you, but I can't take your abuse any longer. If you get the help you need, get sober, and get rid of your demons, I'll be more than happy to be your wife forever. But you do need help, honey."

Pete wrapped his arms around her and sobbed openly. "I'll do it. Just promise you'll stick by me."

A truck pulled into the yard and Jethro Byrd got out. "What the fuck is HE doing here?" Pete yelled.

CHAPTER 29

JETHRO WALKED TENTATIVELY TOWARD Pete and Ed. He glanced at Sawyer and she gave him a nod indicating she was okay. "Hey," he greeted the men. "I heard there was a marine in trouble and thought I'd come by to see if I could help."

"You can help by getting the hell off my property," Pete spat. He attempted to stand up, but Ed pulled him back down onto the steps.

"Cool it, Pete," Ed said.

"I hate that son-of-a bitch," he yelled, shaking his fist at the gunny. "He thinks he's so high and mighty. I always told myself if I ever saw him again I'd beat the shit out of him."

Jethro heard Pete's ranting and was confused. He'd seen Pete in town and at a few meetings, but as far as he knew, he'd never done anything except treat him with respect. He had no idea why Pete was so angry with him.

"You don't even know who I am, do you asshole?" Pete sneered, pointing his finger at Jethro.

"I guess I don't, Pete," Jethro answered. He moved a little closer to the stairs so he could get a better look at him, trying to jog his memory. "Why don't you tell me what I did to make you hate me."

"There you go, getting all sarcastic and cocky, just like you used to. Do you get off on that sense of superiority, Mr.

Byrd? Does it ramp up your ego that you've got your shit together and the rest of us haven't?"

"I don't feel that way at all, Pete. If I sounded sarcastic, I sure didn't mean to. I'm sorry. Actually, I'm feeling bad right now, because our meetings haven't been able to help you.

"Oh, poor Gunny," Pete mocked. "Another misfit in his platoon. Why don't you make me run a few miles in the hot sun, do some pushups until I puke, or some other sadistic punishment for not being as quick to "get it" as the other men. I was only seventeen for chrissake." Pete knew he sounded like a crybaby, but he couldn't help himself.

Jethro was totally puzzled. Had this man been one of his recruits when he was a DI? Surely, he should remember if Pete hated him this much, but there had been so many. He couldn't possibly recall all the men he had instructed.

"Pete. Was I your DI when you enlisted in the corps?" That was the only thing that made sense to Jethro. Many of the men in his squadrons graduated from basic training hating his guts, but if it made them tougher, then he'd done his job.

"Sir, yes, sir," Pete bellowed. He would have stood up and saluted, but Ed wouldn't let go of his shirt.

"I know you feel you have reason to hate me, Pete, but I was teaching you how to be a man, stand on your own two feet so you wouldn't get killed in Iraq. It was my job and whether you hate me or not, I obviously did it right, because here you are. You didn't get killed and you made it home."

All the energy went out of Pete. Spent, scared and emotionally wrecked, he began to cry again. Ed put his arm around his pal's shoulder and patted him on the back.

"It's going to be okay, buddy. We're going to see that you get the help you need."

Pete wiped his nose with the back of his hand. Maddy reached for a hankie in her apron and passed it to her husband. She squatted down beside him and rubbed his back.

"I'm not going anywhere, honey," she spoke softly. "The kids and I will visit and we'll be right here waiting for you when you're well enough to come home."

"I love you, Maddy." Pete laid his head on her chest and she held him tightly.

"Pete," Jethro interrupted. "I need to ask you one more question. When you were in Iraq, were you and the other men given an antimalarial drug?"

Pete ran his hands through his hair, trying to remember. "Oh, yah. I don't know the name of it though. They gave us something and told us to take it weekly. They said it could cause nightmares. Some of us got them, others didn't. Why?"

"The side effects from this drug have been the cause of many men experiencing paranoia, alcoholism, abusing family members, and a number of things. As soon as we get you to the medical center, I'm going to make sure they do an in-depth workup on you. I don't think you have PTSD at all, Pete. I think there's more going on than meets the eye."

Pete looked at Jethro. "Then I'm not just some crazy bastard who hates my drill instructor? There might be a cause for what I've been doing?"

Jethro smiled. "I think so." He turned to Maddy. "Would you pack Pete a small suitcase? We're taking him to Fort Harrison. Okay if I ride along, Pete?"

Pete looked at Ed.

"I could use the company on the ride home," Ed told him. "Jethro can explain this better than I can, so I think we could use his help."

Pete hesitated before responding. "If that's what you think, Ed, okay."

Jethro walked over to Sawyer. "Let George know what's going on. I'll be back later."

She didn't question him, just nodded and let out a heavy sigh. She was so glad no one got hurt and it had ended amicably. For a few minutes, she was afraid she might have to use her gun. The standoff reminded her of police negotiations she'd witnessed in Florida when a former marine had barricaded himself and his wife in their house. It hadn't ended as well as today. The marine killed his wife and then turned the gun on himself. She wondered now if that marine had taken the same drug that Pete took. She planned to look into it further and pass the word along to her police friends back in Orlando.

AFTER THE MEN LEFT for Fort. Harrison, Sawyer went into the house with Maddy. She wanted to make sure Maddy was fine before getting back to the station. "You going to be all right?" she asked.

"It's such a relief to have him gone. He's been like a crazy person for the past several months, getting worse every day. I don't even know the man they just took away, and that makes me so sad." Maddy began to weep.

Sawyer put her arms around her and held her tightly, letting her cry. "You're a strong woman. I can't imagine how difficult it's been for you lately. Watching him turn into a totally different person has to be very scary."

Maddy dropped down in a kitchen chair and rested her head on her hands. She took a breath and looked up at Sawyer. "Everything he's done is totally out of character. You don't know the real Pete. He's a great man, loving, funny, a good father, and a good cop. That's why George has been so lenient. He's been like a father to Pete, but he's also Pete's boss so eventually he had to put him on leave."

"Is there anything I can do for you before I head back to town?"

"Would you stay for a little bit, have a coffee or tea; let me unwind a little before the kids get home?"

"I sure will. I'll give George a call to let him know what's going on. Why don't you put the kettle on while I make my call?"

"Thank you, Deputy."

"Why don't you call me Sawyer," she smiled.

Maddy's eyes filled with tears. "Thanks, Sawyer. Maybe

someday we can be friends."

"I'd like that. Let me call George, and I'll get right back to you."

"Okay."

"SHERIFF'S OFFICE," VIVIAN BROWN said answering the call.

"Hi, Viv. It's Sawyer. Is the sheriff there?"

"Hold on. He's outside shooting the breeze with someone. I'll go get him."

Sawyer smiled at the informality of her current employment. Life in Stony Creek had its ups and downs, but she'd take this any day over the current crime wave in Orlando.

"Sawyer. Where the hell have you been?" George barked into the phone.

"I'm with Maddy. Ed and Jethro have taken Pete over to Fort Harrison to the VA Medical Center. It was a bit uncomfortable when I first got out there, but Ed and Jethro knew just how to handle Pete and got everything under control." She didn't tell George how afraid she was about the possibility of having to use her gun. *You don't have to tell everything you know*, she told herself.

"Is Maddy okay?" he worried.

"She is now. She wants me to stay for a little while and have a cup of tea with her. Would that be okay, or do you need me to come right back?"

"You stay as long as she needs you."

"Jethro thinks that Pete might have been issued some antimalarial drug which has been causing a multitude of problems for some of the men who took it. He doesn't think Pete has PTSD, but his behavior could be from this drug."

"How could that be? Pete's been home from Iraq for eight years. He did have an alcohol problem and smoked pot, but had it under control, or so I thought."

"I don't know much about it myself. Ed and Jethro will fill you in when they get back. I just hope the VA will admit him. He doesn't have an appointment, so they're going over there on a wing and a prayer."

"The VA can blue paper Pete if they think he's a harm to someone or to himself. There are ways of getting around things if you push hard enough. Take your time and I'll see you back here in a while."

"Thanks, George. Call me if you need me."

"You can count on it."

CHAPTER 30

BEFORE LEAVING TOWN, THE three men stopped by Elliott's office for a referral. Ed briefly filled him in on what had transpired that morning. After a hasty checkup and a few questions, Elliott signed a form stating that in his professional opinion, Pete should be admitted to the hospital.

Once they were on their way, Pete fell asleep in the backseat, snoring loudly on the three-hour ride to Fort Harrison. Ed and Jethro talked quietly so as not to awaken their friend.

"Thanks for the help this morning," Ed said. "I wasn't sure what I was going to find when I got out there. My main concern was keeping Sawyer and Maddy safe."

Jethro nodded. "I have a police scanner at the house so I heard the call. Pete had been coming to meetings, reluctantly, but he was there nevertheless. I figured I'd try to help if I could. I had no idea he had all that animosity toward me. He's never said a word until today."

"When he saw you get out of the truck, I thought he was going to blow a gasket. Good thing he didn't have a weapon, because, at that moment, I'm not sure what he would have done."

"I don't think he's a killer, but I'm glad we didn't have to find out. I hope the doctors at the VA will be able to figure out what's ailing him."

"Yeah, me too. He's not the same man I've known all my life. Can I ask you a personal question?"

"Yup, but I can't guarantee I'll answer. Depends on what it is."

"You sweet on Sawyer?"

Jethro shrugged.

"Well, she's a good girl. I'd hate to see her get hurt."

"No need to worry about that."

"Good."

Jethro leaned forward and turned on the radio. His way of changing the subject. They rode the rest of the way in silence.

SAWYER HUGGED MADDY WHEN she was ready to head back to town. "You gonna' be okay?" she asked, looking at her intently.

"I'll be fine if I can just stop crying. I'm fine one minute, and the next I'm blubbering all over again." Maddy brushed her hair from her face and tucked a strand behind her ear. "I know I have to pull myself together before the kids get home from school," she answered. Her eyes welled up and her chin wobbled a little.

"I can stay a while longer if you want me to," Sawyer assured her. She put her arm around Maddy's shoulder and led her toward the kitchen. "Hey, I know what. How about we bake some cookies for Molly and Jackson?" She licked her lips. "Yum, nice warm cookies right out of the oven and a cold glass of milk. Sounds so good I think I'm going to stay." She laughed.

Maddy grinned. "That's a great idea. The kids will love it. Chocolate chip?" she asked, opening the pantry door.

"Oh yeah, my favorite. Please let me help. I need to become a little more domestic."

"Oh, why's that?" Maddy asked, cocking an eyebrow. She had heard through the grapevine that the young deputy was seeing Jethro Byrd.

Her mouth kicked in before her brain and she answered, “If I told you, then I’d have to kill you.” The minute the words were out of her mouth, she wanted to cut out her tongue. They seemed to hang in mid-air like a hummingbird at a feeder. She hurried across the kitchen and grabbed Maddy’s hands. “Oh my God, I am so sorry. After what you’ve been through today, I come out with a stupid remark like that. Please forgive me.”

Maddy stared at her for what seemed to Sawyer like eternity, and then she burst out laughing. All the tension she’d been feeling the past several months washed away in one hearty laugh.

Sawyer stifled a giggle and then began laughing, too. Before long, tears were running down their cheeks. One round of laughter louder than the next.

Maddy finally sank down onto a chair holding her belly. “I needed that, thanks. I haven’t felt this good in…I don’t know when,” she said.

Relieved that her faux pas didn’t throw Maddy over the edge, Sawyer continued to chuckle in between hiccups and gasping for breath. “That was so bad of me,” she said, and she began to laugh again.

Maddy put her hand over her heart. “I wish you could have seen your face,” she giggled. “I’ve never seen anything funnier. I thought for sure you were going to throw up. All the color drained out and all I could see was your big, bulging blue eyes.” She wheezed with laughter.

Sawyer fanned her face with a napkin and tried to compose herself. As bad as the day began, this afternoon was perfect. *This woman is going to be one of my best friends. I just know it. How I’ve missed girlfriend time since I’ve been here.*

“I guess we better get working on those cookies or the kids will be home before we know it.” Maddy said. “The bowls are in that cupboard over there,” she pointed the way while she was gathering up spoons and measuring cups from a kitchen drawer.

Sawyer retrieved the bowls and under Maddy's watchful tutorage, she made her first batch of cookies.

WITH HER BELLY FULL OF chocolate chip cookies, Sawyer headed back to town to check in with George. The children had been delighted with their treat. Maddy had given her the recipe so she could try to make the cookies on her own.

As she drove, she smiled and felt good about the day. Pete was getting help, no one had been hurt, and she hoped Maddy and the children would be able to get back to normal while he was away.

Thunder pulsed in the distance and the sky turned a gunmetal gray. The wind picked up and rain began falling in large drops. She activated the windshield wipers, turned the cruiser around and headed for her house to pick up Cooper. She hated storms and her little dog would be company for her.

The rain was coming down in sheets when she got to the house. She covered her head with her jacket and ran across the yard. Inside, Cooper was lying on his bed in the kitchen and didn't seem concerned about the storm at all. "Hey there, Coop," she said leaning down to pat him on the head.

Cooper thumped his tail and rolled over on his back displaying his tummy for a rub.

Sawyer looked down at him and smiled, marveling at how fast he was growing. He was a handsome boy. His body was a beautiful black and tan with two brown feet and two white. His muzzle was partly white, and he had black rings around his eyes that looked like a mask. Whenever she looked at him, she thought she should have named him Bandit.

Cooper had a sweet disposition. Sawyer had no trouble socializing him with other dogs, including Meredith and Dakota's Tripp and Bill, and, of course, Mabel, who thought she was his mother.

"Come on, boy, get up. We have work to do. George is waiting for us." She tugged on his collar; reluctantly he stood up and shook himself. "Want to go see George?" Cooper wagged his tail in agreement and headed for the door.

AN HOUR LATER, SAWYER walked into the office. George was just hanging up the phone, a worried expression on his face.

"What's wrong?" she asked.

He cleared his throat before speaking. "That was the VA Medical Center, a Doctor Mason. Pete still had a lot of alcohol in his system, so they didn't do a blood panel on him. But, they did order an MRI because he was complaining of severe headaches." George paused.

Sawyer sat down facing him before he went on. Cooper went over and laid his chin on George's lap. Absentmindedly, he stroked the young dog's head.

"The news isn't good, I'm afraid, but it does explain a lot. Pete has a brain tumor. They want to operate as soon as they can. Probably in a couple of days."

"Why don't they do it now?" she asked.

"He's so full of booze they don't want to put him under unless it becomes an emergency. If that happens, then they'll do what they have to do."

Sawyer was curious. "Do they think it's malignant?"

"They won't know until they operate. I sure hope not."

"Do you mind if I tell Maddy?"

"I'd appreciate it if you would. She might cry, and I never know what do to when a woman starts crying. Have you heard from Ed and Jethro?"

"I talked to Ed," she said. They're staying at the hospital for a while. Pete's been given a mild sedative so he can sleep. He doesn't know about the tumor. Ed wants to tell him."

"Okay. I'll head out to Maddy's."

"If I can help, let me know."

"I'll be fine. Maddy is a tough cookie. She might even be relieved knowing why Pete's behavior has been so irrational. Hopefully, his condition is treatable."

"Why don't you go on home when you're done? It's been a long day."

"Thanks. I will. I'll see you in the morning. Come on, Cooper."

George reached in the middle drawer of his desk. Cooper's eyes sparkled. Cookie time.

Sawyer scowled. "George," she scolded.

George leaned down and whispered in Cooper's ear. "Don't pay her no mind. Hurry up and eat the cookie. Why don't you leave him with me? I'll take him home and bring him to work tomorrow."

"You sure you want to do that?"

"Go get Maddy. Coop and I will be just fine, won't we boy," he said.

Cooper let out a big sigh and slid down on the floor beside George.

As Sawyer let herself out, she bet Coop was just waiting for her to leave so he could have more cookies.

CHAPTER 31

MADDY WAS SITTING ON the top step of the porch, twisting a hankie into tear filled knots, when Sawyer pulled into the driveway. The worry on her face was unmistakable.

The deputy parked the cruiser and got out. "You heard?" she asked, walking across the yard and up the steps.

Maddy nodded. "The doctor called. Said Pete has a brain tumor and they need to operate." Tears streamed down her cheeks.

Sawyer sat down, covered one of Maddy's hands with her own and gave a gentle squeeze. "It's going to be okay."

Maddy raised a shaky hand and dabbed her tears with the hankie. "I don't want him to die," she swallowed a sob.

"Pete's in the right place to get the best care. I know you're afraid, but I don't think he's going to die. At least now you know the reason he's been acting the way he has. This wasn't his fault at all."

"But what if it's malignant? I don't think he'll be able to handle it, chemo, radiation, and all. He'll end up shooting himself."

Sawyer felt for her friend and hoped she could find the right words to make Maddy feel better. "You have every right to be concerned, but let's not borrow trouble. The unknown is the scary part, so let's take it one step at a time. When will you be going to the hospital?"

"As soon as I can. I have to find a sitter for the kids first. I don't even know how to get to the VA." Maddy cried silently and put her head in her hands.

The screen door flung open and Molly and Jackson came running out onto the porch. "Momma, can we go see Daddy now?" Molly asked, a half-eaten chocolate chip cookie melting in her hand.

Maddy sat upright, turned her face away and wiped her tears. Turning back to the children, she gave them a reassuring smile. "You kids can't go see him for a few days, but Momma has to go and sign some papers. Daddy's sick and needs an operation."

"What's the matter with him?" Jackson asked, sticking his thumb in his mouth. Pete hated it when he did that, often called him a baby, but Maddy saw how this simple act comforted Jackson when he was worried or upset.

"He has something wrong inside his head and the doctors are going to fix it. Then Daddy can come back home." She hugged him tightly. Maddy didn't want to tell them more than they'd be able to understand. Jackson was only seven and Molly was nine. Better to keep things as simple as possible for now.

Sawyer watched the interaction between a mother and her children. One minute she was crying and scared about the outcome of Pete's surgery, but as soon as her children came out to the porch, her whole demeanor changed. She was calm and smiling, reassuring Jackson and his sister that everything was going to be okay. Sawyer marveled at her maternal strength.

"Maddy, why don't you take the kids inside? I have a couple of calls to make and I'll be right back." She ran down the steps to the cruiser.

Sawyer called George and told him what was going on. They decided she should take Maddy to the VA because, in her emotional state, it wasn't safe for her to make the drive by herself.

"Is she taking the kids with her?" George asked.

"That's not a good idea. I thought I'd call Elliott and ask him if he would watch them until we got back. The kids would have someone to play with. What do you think?"

"It's worth a try. If he can't do it, call my wife. I'm sure she'll offer to help."

"Okay. I'll call you later." She disconnected the call and dialed Elliott's number.

After a couple of rings, he picked up. "Doc Webster."

"Elliott, this is Sawyer. I have a favor to ask."

"I'm all ears. What's up?"

"Maddy Tucker needs to go to the VA Medical Center to see Pete. He has a brain tumor and they need to operate as soon as he's stable."

"That's terrible, but it sure explains a lot. What do you want me to do?"

"Will you watch her kids while I take her over to Fort Harrison? I thought if they could hang out with Davy and Doug and have some fun it might take their minds off their father."

"Sure, but if an emergency comes up I might have to leave, but I have some high school girls who babysit for me. Will Maddy be okay with that?"

"I'm sure she will, but I'll double check just to be on the safe side. I'll be back later on to take the kids to my house for the night. They have school tomorrow, so between all of us, we can work out something until Maddy gets home."

"Where are you now?"

"At the Tucker's. We should be there within the hour, if that's okay."

"I'll be here. I know the boys will enjoy the company."

"Thanks, Elliott. I owe you one."

"Hey, don't even get me started on that," he chuckled.

MADDY AND SAWYER WAITED for Dr. Mason at the

reception desk. “I’m so nervous I feel sick to my stomach,” Maddy said, wrapping her arms around her middle.

“You’re going to be just fine,” Sawyer encouraged her. “I think you probably know most of the news anyway, so this will be just a matter of reviewing and signing paperwork for Pete’s surgery.”

“What if he doesn’t want the surgery? What should I do?” She paced back and forth in front of the desk, glancing at a clock on the wall. “Where is that doctor anyway?”

“I guess you’ll have to try to reassure Pete that it’s for the best so he can get well. Let’s sit down while we wait. I’m sure the doctor will be here soon.” Sawyer pointed to a bench along the wall. She was afraid Maddy might pass out.

Several minutes later, an older man wearing green scrubs introduced himself. “Mrs. Tucker, I’m Doctor Mason.”

The first thing Maddy noticed was his long, salt n’ pepper handlebar moustache, and then his kind smile. When she attempted to stand, he motioned for her to sit and took a seat beside her.

“I know this is a very scary time for you right now, but I believe surgery is of the utmost importance for Pete to not only survive, but to return to the man you used to know. It’ll be an uphill battle and he’ll need some rehab, but within a year he should be back to normal.”

Maddy had been holding her breath the whole time Dr. Mason was speaking. She felt like she was in a trance, where none of this was really happening. When he finished, she exhaled loudly, as if all the life was draining out of her. Did he say uphill battle, rehab, and a year before Pete would be better? How was she going to explain all that to him? He’d never agree to it. She knew her husband.

“Mrs. Tucker, are you all right?” Dr. Mason gently touched her arm.

Maddy looked at the doctor, her expression tense and uncertain. She shook her head. “Pete will never agree to the operation if I tell him what you just said. He’ll sign himself out of here, and God only knows what will happen." She started trembling just thinking about it.

Sawyer reached over and held Maddy's hand.

"Well, you're right about him being able to sign himself out," Dr. Mason said, "but we've got him for another 48 hours before he can do that."

Maddy looked confused.

"When we blue-paper a person, meaning when we admit someone without their consent, we can keep them 72 hours for evaluation. Pete hasn't been here 24 hours yet, so we have time to get him to see it our way."

Mumbling, Maddy shook her head. "I know he'll never agree. Is the tumor malignant?"

"I don't think so. These types of tumors are usually benign, but we won't know for sure until we're in there. It is lying near an area that controls motor skills, which is why I said he'd need some rehab. All surgeries come with risk, but I'll do my best."

"Those don't sound like very good odds, doctor. I can't make this decision for Pete. He has to do it. He'll never forgive me if I sign the papers and he ends up in a wheelchair or worse. I just can't do it. I won't." Maddy began to cry softly.

"Would you like to go see Pete now?" Dr. Mason asked. "He's awake, but he's got one heck of a hangover."

Maddy's stomach tightened and she stood on shaky legs. "I have to see him sometime, so I guess now is as good as ever."

She and Sawyer followed Dr. Mason down a long hallway. The air smelled of bleach and antiseptic. They whispered to each other, assuming they were on the surgical wing from all the cries and moans they heard as they made their way to Pete's room. Dr. Mason stopped in front of a doorway. "Ladies," he said, stepping aside for them to enter the room.

"You go ahead, Maddy," Sawyer told her. "I'll be right

outside if you need me."

Maddy nodded and cautiously peeked into the dimly lit room. Pete had an IV drip attached to one arm and his hands were restrained to the bed rails. He lay silently, looking like death warmed over. Ed and Jethro were sitting on either side of him, talking quietly. They looked up when they saw Maddy.

"Maddy, come on in," Ed said. He stood and motioned for her to sit in the chair beside Pete.

Maddy hesitated, dreading that she would have to tell Pete about the tumor.

Ed went over to her, put one hand on her elbow and another around her waist. He led her toward her husband. "He's pretty much been in and out of it for hours. I think knowing you're here will make him feel better."

Maddy whispered. "I don't know how I'm going to tell him he has a brain tumor and needs surgery."

"I've already told him, Maddy. He took it about as well as you would expect…not so good. It'll be up to you to convince him to have the operation."

Maddy looked over at her husband. Her heart went out to him. She wished she could take away his pain, but she had little left to give to make him feel better. She took a seat beside Pete and rested her hand on his forearm. "Pete. I'm here, honey." She smoothed the blond hairs on his arm and leaned in to kiss his hand.

Pete's fingers twitched and after a few minutes, he opened his eyes. "Maddy, is it really you?" His eyes welled up.

"I'm right here, Pete. How do you feel?"

"Not so good. Would you ask the nurse to untie my hands so I can touch you?"

"I can't do that, hon. As soon as you're feeling better, they'll take the restraints off." Maddy noticed a vein in Pete's forehead start to bulge, a sure sign he was getting agitated. His fingers clenched into fists; afraid, she pushed her chair back away from the bed.

Ed walked over to Pete. "You okay, buddy?"

Pete glared at them. "Both of you get the hell out of here," he shouted. "I don't need you. As soon as they get these ties off me, I'm signing myself out."

"Pete, you can't come home right now because you need an operation. You have a brain tumor and could die." Maddy felt a trickle of dread. Pete could be downright stubborn and when he set his mind to something, it was hard to change. Their saving grace was the hospital didn't have to release him for two more days. Maybe in that time, Pete would change his mind.

As Maddy stood to leave, Pete began acting erratically. His body was posturing and he was in a full-blown seizure within seconds. Jethro and Ed held his legs so he wouldn't hurt himself, while Maddy ran to the hallway. "Help, please, my husband is having a seizure."

The nurses came running and shooed everyone out of the room. Someone on the intercom system paged Dr. Mason, STAT. He magically appeared and ran into Pete's room. There was a flurry of activity; within minutes, they rushed Pete into the hall on a gurney.

"We have to operate immediately, Mrs. Tucker. Please sign the papers. It's out of Pete's hands now." He grabbed onto a bed railing and began to push. "Let's get this man to the OR!" he ordered the nurses.

Maddy looked at her three friends and they nodded.

"Here you go, Mrs. Tucker," the nurse said, handing her some paperwork and a pen. "I've highlighted the three places you need to sign."

She glanced at them and with shaking hand signed, *Madeline Wilson Tucker*. Pete's future was literally in her hands, whatever it may be.

CHAPTER 32

HOURS LATER, DR. MASON left the OR. He pulled off his surgical cap and used it to wipe sweat from his brow. He walked down the long hallway toward the waiting room. He hated this part of his job. No matter how many times he had to deliver bad news, it didn't get any easier.

Standing outside the double doors, he took a deep breath before entering the room. What he was about to say would change Mrs. Tucker's and her children's lives forever, so he wanted to choose his words wisely.

He pushed the doors open and everyone looked up at him expectantly. The surgeon slowly shook his head and began to speak. "I'm afraid I have some really sad news for you."

From the doctor's demeanor, they knew Pete hadn't made it. Ed put his arm around Maddy as she covered her mouth to stifle a sob. Jethro and Sawyer moved their chairs closer to Maddy before the doctor spoke again.

Dr. Mason sat down in a chair facing her and went on. "Mrs. Tucker. As you know, Pete had a brain tumor. Despite our best efforts, he died during surgery."

Maddy burst into tears. "I never should have signed those papers! He'd still be alive if I hadn't. This is all my fault. He's going to hate me for this." Even as she spoke the words, Maddy knew how crazy she sounded. Pete couldn't hate her. Pete was dead.

“Mrs. Tucker. This is no one’s fault,” Dr. Mason explained. “Pete’s brain tumor was much larger than expected and had spread to other areas. If he had lived, he would have been in a vegetative state for the rest of his life. Neither of you would have wanted that.”

“You’re right,” Maddy sobbed, “but somehow I still feel responsible.”

“If it’ll ease your mind, we can do an autopsy,” the doctor told her, “but I don’t think it will change the outcome. He died from a brain tumor, plain and simple.”

Ed squeezed Maddy’s shoulder. “Better to have people know that, Maddy, than anything else,” he told her. “Better for Molly and Jackson, too.”

“If there’s anything we can do to help you, please don’t hesitate to contact us. This hospital has a wonderful support team at the ready if you need help with arrangements and all.”

Maddy shook her head. “Could I see my husband, please?”

“Of course. Give us a few minutes and I’ll come back and take you to him.”

IT WAS NEAR DAWN before they left the hospital. Maddy had said her good-byes to her husband with Ed at her side. As sad as he felt losing his best friend, he had to be strong for her.

The ride back to Stony Creek was solemn. Maddy rode with Ed, and Sawyer and Jethro followed behind. Ed put in a quick call to George.

“Sheriff Logan,” George barked into the phone. He’d been awake all night worrying about Pete.

“George,” Ed said. “The news isn’t good. Pete didn’t make it through the surgery. The tumor had spread. They did all they could, but it wasn’t good enough.”

“Oh man, that sucks.” George loved Pete like a son and the news broke his heart. “Hold on a sec.” He sat up, grabbed a Kleenex from the nightstand and blew his nose. He wiped tears from his eyes before speaking again. "How's Maddy?"

"She's holding up as well as can be expected. She wants to pick up her kids and take them home, so we're on the way to Elliott's."

"Get some rest and come to the office when you can. If I need you, I'll call. Where's Sawyer?"

"She's on her way home to freshen up."

"It's been a long night for both of you. Take as much time as you need and I'll see you when you get here."

"George?"

"Yeah?"

"This was tough."

"I know, Ed. See you later."

Abby rolled over and saw George sitting on the side of the bed, head in his hands. "What happened?" She sat up and wrapped her arms around his back. "Talk to me, Georgie."

"Pete didn't make it."

"Oh honey, I'm so sorry. I know how much he meant to you."

George stood up and ran his hands through his hair. "Guess we need to help Maddy make funeral arrangements."

Abby nodded. "I'll pay her a visit this morning to see how we can assist her."

LATER THAT MORNING, ED arrived at the station after a few hours rest. George was sitting at his desk looking sad and forlorn, Cooper lying at his feet. "How you holding up?" Ed asked him.

"I feel helpless. Feels like I should be doing something and here I sit doing nothing." He paused before going on. "You know, Ed, now that Pete's gone I'll have to hire another deputy, and right soon. There's too much territory for the three of us to handle."

"You're right. We've been fortunate no one has called or

needed us with an emergency. We both know that's not going to last."

"I wonder if Jethro would consider the job."

"I doubt it," Ed said. "He has a lot going on with his ranch and mentoring the men. And now he's sweet on Sawyer; I doubt it would work."

"I guess you're right."

Trying to relax the situation, Ed said, "Hey, if you hire someone online again, make sure you check out whether they're male or female." He laughed at George's scowl.

By the time Vivian came into work, the whole town knew of Pete's passing. Being a dispatcher in a small town had its advantages. She was the town crier and everyone knew it. If you wanted to know something, ask Vivian. "Morning guys," she said, placing a box of muffins on George's desk. "I have a feeling it's going to be a busy day. I'll make some fresh coffee."

Cooper jumped up from under George's chair, began barking and wagging his tail. He ran to the backdoor just as it opened and Sawyer came in. "Hey, boy." She squatted and hugged her dog. "Did you have a good sleepover with George and Abby?" She rubbed his ears and Cooper licked her face. "Good. I'm glad you had a good time. Now let's get to work."

Sawyer grabbed a cup of coffee and walked into the office. "How's it going, guys?"

"Doing okay. Ed and I were talking about hiring a new deputy. We don't have enough help."

"Make sure you know whether you're hiring a male or female this time," she snickered.

"For the love of God!" George stuffed his hat on his head and stood up. "I'm going out to the diner for some peace and quiet, and a decent cup of coffee." He looked squarely at Vivian.

"You sure got your long johns in a bunch. Probably best you do take a ride," she quipped.

"Humph!" George opened the door and slammed it on his

way out.

"I probably shouldn't have said that," Vivian remarked after George left. "I was trying to lighten the mood, but….."

"We all were, Viv," Ed interrupted. "He knows how we feel. He needs to let off a little steam, that's all."

The three of them knew the sheriff was grieving silently and their hearts ached for him.

ABBY LOGAN DROVE OUT to the Tucker place to see what she could do for Maddy. She parked in the driveway, removed a crockpot from the back seat, and made her way up the porch steps. She rapped on the door and waited.

Maddy peeked out through the curtains and opened the door. "Mrs. Logan. How good to see you," she said. "Come in, please."

Abby couldn't help but notice Maddy's red eyes and dark circles. She looked exhausted, and she was probably hungry. "I'm so sorry about Pete," she told her, which brought on a deluge of tears. Abby put her arms around Maddy and hugged her. "It's all right, sweetie. Let it go. It's better to let it out than hold it in. Do the children know?"

Maddy nodded.

"How are they doing?

"They're doing okay. They know their daddy is in heaven with their Nana and Grandpa."

"There's a roast and some veggies in the crockpot. All you have to do is plug it in and it'll be ready in about four hours." She set the slow cooker on the counter. "You won't be alone through all this. Trust me. George and I will do everything we can to help get Pete's benefit papers in order, make arrangements for the funeral, and whatever else you might need."

"Thank you so much, Mrs. Logan." Maddy gave the older woman a hug. She felt like a hundred pounds were off her shoulders.

OVER THE NEXT FEW days, the town's people rallied around Maddy Tucker and her children. The women came by with meals, offered to run errands or take care of the children, while the men mowed the front lawn and made repairs that Pete hadn't gotten around to doing. Overwhelmed by their generosity, Maddy often reduced to tears. She didn't know how she could ever repay everyone.

ON A BRIGHT, SUNNY morning, Maddy laid her husband to rest in the Stony Creek Cemetery alongside his parents. A few deputies from surrounding counties arrived to show support. Reverend Storm Anderson presided over the funeral and delivered a eulogy that would have pleased Pete. Deputy Tucker was finally at peace.

AFTER THE RECEPTION AT the Grange Hall, Maddy thanked everyone, and after saying her good-byes, she took her children home. There was a lot on her mind and she had decisions to make.

Once home, Maddy told the kids, "Momma needs a little time to think. How about you go watch television while I have a cup of coffee. Later on, we can make ice cream sundaes. How does that sound?"

"Yea!" they yelled. "Can I have chocolate sauce on mine?" Molly asked.

"Can I have vanilla ice cream and nuts?" her little brother wanted to know.

"Give me a little while to relax, and you can make your sundaes anyway you want them." She smiled at her children as they ran into the living room.

Maddy poured herself a steaming cup of coffee and sat at the kitchen table. She stared out the window, remembering all the hopes and dreams she and Pete had for this place. It certainly hadn't turned out the way they had planned. Those hopes and dreams were dead now. Maddy took a sip from her cup and knew what she had to do. She picked up the phone and dialed.

"Hello. Nola Cummings here. How can I help you?"

CHAPTER 33

COOPER JUMPED INTO THE patrol car and climbed onto the back seat. “Good boy,” Sawyer said, and rewarded him with a pat on the head. “Let’s go see Mabel.” Cooper’s tail thumped up and down in response.

She needed to see Jethro, have him hold her in his arms. He somehow had a way of making all the bad go away. As she bumped along the gravel road, her thoughts turned to the events of the past month. Things had been stressful at the office ever since Pete’s death. George hadn’t been himself, which put everyone on edge. He’d borrowed a deputy from Custer County, Cole Bradford, who wasn’t happy about the temporary transfer. He made it known to anyone who would listen that he wanted to get back home as soon as possible. Sawyer wanted things to go back to normal, too, but it seemed it was going to take a while.

She pulled into Jethro’s driveway, stopped and opened the cruiser door for Cooper. He jumped out and ran down the hill, barking and wagging his tail in sheer happiness. Mabel ran to greet him. Sawyer couldn’t help but smile as she watched the interaction between the two dogs. They ran around like kindergartners at recess, bounding after a ball, and barking playfully.

Jethro came out onto the porch to investigate the ruckus. He’d been out back and hadn’t heard Sawyer pull into the yard. He waved. His heart skipped a beat every time he saw her. She was beautiful, sexy, playful, independent, but most of all, and the best part, she loved him. "Hey," he said, a charming, lop-sided grin on his face.

"Hey, yourself," she smiled back at him. "Got a minute?"

He walked down the steps and put his arms around her. "I've got all the time in the world for you, my sweet. What's up?"

She relaxed against his body and laid her head on his chest. "I just needed to see you this morning." He smelled so good and she wrapped her arms tighter around his waist. She had a distinctive tingle in her belly whenever she was close to him. Kind of like a cat in heat…all the time. She pressed a little closer to him.

"Hey woman, it's only been a couple of days," he teased, giving her a quick pat on her butt.

"Don't be so sure of yourself," she said, and pulled away from him. "You got coffee?"

"I do. Want some?"

She gave him an exasperated look and started up the steps to the house. She turned and looked back at him. "You coming?"

Jethro's eyes twinkled and he wiggled his eyebrows up and down. "I plan to." He hurried up the steps and grabbed her around the waist.

Sawyer squealed and pretended to fight him off as he picked her up in his arms, entered the house and headed for the bedroom. "This is not what I came over here for," she lied.

"I know. You wanted coffee."

"I still do, but I guess it can wait a while."

"Waiting makes it all the better," he whispered, as he released her from his arms and stood her before him. He undid the buttons of her blouse and reached inside her bra. He cupped her breasts and stroked her nipples with his thumb, leaning in to kiss one and then the other. He settled his mouth on hers in a long, passionate kiss, tongues intermingling and hearts pounding against each other.

"I need you, Jethro," Sawyer whispered, leading him toward the bed.

"Me, too, babe."

SATISFIED AND RELAXED AFTER lovemaking, they sat in the kitchen drinking coffee. Mabel and Cooper planked themselves under the table with loud sighs. Sawyer looked at Jethro and a slow smile spread across his face. "That was really nice, and unexpected." He reached out and held her hand.

A pink flush stained her cheeks. "I really didn't come over for that, but I don't suppose you believe me."

Jethro noticed the blush. "I prefer to think you were lusting after my body and couldn't control yourself."

"In your dreams, sweetheart. In your dreams."

"It's all I dream about," he quipped, then laughed.

"Do you have anything to eat?" she asked.

He shot her a sexy grin and raised an eyebrow. "What would you like?"

She cuffed him on the arm. "You are such a pig. How about some toast or a muffin, something to sustain me for a few hours. I have to go to work."

"And I thought you were going to spend the day. You used me for your own pleasure and now you're going to leave. Humph! I've heard about girls like you." He slid his chair back and went to the refrigerator, hiding a grin after seeing the expression on her face at his comment.

Sawyer's cell phone rang. "Deputy Mackenzie."

It was Sadie. "Hi, sweetie. Would you stop by sometime today? I'm planning a surprise baby shower for Meredith and need some help organizing." She didn't really need the help, but she missed having Sawyer around since she moved out. This was a good excuse to spend some time together.

"I'd love to. Will you be home all day? I'm working, but I'll get out there when I can."

"I'll be right here. It'll be good to spend a little time with you and chat. I've missed you. I just made some apple and blueberry muffins and need help eating them up before Charlie gets his hands on them."

"Looking forward to it. I'll see you in a while."

"Okay, bye." Sadie disconnected the call.

"That was Sadie," Sawyer said.

"Everything okay with her and Charlie?" he asked, placing a plate with a blueberry muffin and slice of cheese in front of her.

She looked up at him. "That looks wonderful, thanks."

"Anything for m'lady," he said, bowing.

"Now that's the kind of man I want right there," she giggled.

NOLA CUMMINGS KNOCKED ON Maddy Tucker's front door. While she waited, she took a note of the surroundings, mentally assessing the value of the property. Large house, barn, several outbuildings, acreage, but devoid of any livestock that she could see. That seemed strange. Just as she was about to knock again, the door opened and Maddy greeted her with a warm smile.

"Ms. Cummings, please come in." Maddy stood aside as the realtor entered. She couldn't help but notice her clothes and hair. She looked like she had just stepped out of one those high-priced stores in Bozeman.

Nola wore a bright pink zebra-striped blouse, black jeans with white Aztec embroidery on the back pockets, and black boots. Her chestnut hair, braided to the side, hung loosely over her shoulder. Maddy felt dowdy in her plaid, faded housedress, which was outdated and hung on her like a burlap sack. She had lost a lot of weight over the past several months.

Nola turned to Maddy. “Please accept my condolences for your loss. I know this must be a difficult time for you and the children.”

Maddy’s eyes filled with tears and she nodded.

“Shall we do this another time?” Nola asked. “Maybe it’s too soon.”

“No, I want to do this now.” Maddy asked, “Would you like something to drink? Let’s go in the kitchen and talk things over.”

“Nothing for me thanks, but I would like to hear your ideas and plans.”

Maddy led Nola to the kitchen. “Have a seat,” she said. “You sure I can’t get you something?”

“I’m sure.” Nola sat down, pulled some paperwork from her briefcase and laid it on the table.

Maddy poured herself a glass of water and took a seat beside Nola. “I want to sell everything.”

“Everything? Even the furniture? What do you plan to do after that? I know it’s none of my business, but your husband hasn’t been gone that long. I’d hate to have you do something you might regret later.”

“There’s no way I want to stay here. Too many memories and a lot of them bad. The kids and I need a fresh start.”

“Where will you go?”

“I want to stay in Stony Creek. If this place sells, *when* this place sells,” she corrected, “I’ll buy a little house in town. Could you be my realtor for that, too?”

“I can, if you’re sure that’s what you want.” Nola shifted in her chair and pulled a pen from her briefcase. “Now, tell me about this property, and all that goes with it. Then I can do a comparative analysis with a figure that will sell everything. Hopefully, it’ll be enough for you and the kids to start over.”

For the next two hours, the women walked the property, went through the outbuildings and lastly the house. “What happened to all the livestock?” Nola asked.

“Pete got rid of all the animals. That’s all you need to

know." She turned her face and swatted away a tear.

Nola left it at that, and didn't press Maddy for more information. She took pictures, taking careful note of what Maddy told her about the property. She felt sorry for her. According to local gossip, she had survived an abusive relationship and Nola wanted to help her get a fresh start.

"Well, I think I have all I need to get us started. I'll call back in a couple of days with a fair price. If you agree, we'll get it on the market."

"Thanks so much, Ms. Cummings. I'll be waiting to hear from you."

"Please, call me Nola. We'll be spending time together," she said, giving Maddy a light pat on her shoulder, "so let's keep it simple, shall we?" She smiled sweetly and turned to leave.

Maddy thought the tone of Nola's voice had changed and sounded somewhat condescending, but decided to let it go for now. She didn't need to make any enemies when she needed all the help she could get.

What Maddy hadn't disclosed to Nola was that they were five payments behind in the mortgage. The bank had threatened foreclosure if she didn't catch up.

CHAPTER 34

MIKE BISHOP KNOCKED ON Jethro Byrd's back door. Bonnie, his black Catahoula dog, waited patiently by his side. For the past several weeks, Mike had been rehearsing what he wanted to propose to the gunny, hoping he would understand and support him.

"It's open," Jethro hollered. "Mabel, stay," he ordered, when she stood up to investigate.

Mike let himself in. "Boss. Where you at?"

"In the living room. Come on in."

"Hey," Mike said, as he entered the room. "Mind if I sit down?"

"Take a load off," Jethro answered, jerking his chin toward a chair. "Can I get you a coffee or soft drink?" He picked up the remote control and turned off the television.

"I'll have a cola," Mike said, sitting down in a deep leather chair. His mouth was dry as a bone. Bonnie laid down beside him.

Jethro got up from the couch and went to the kitchen.

Mike was jumpy as spit on a hot skillet. While waiting for his boss to return, perspiration formed on his forehead as he considered the words he might say to the gunny. Mike sat up straighter in the chair when he heard the refrigerator door open and close, and then footsteps coming back into the room.

Jethro handed him the soda. "Problem?"

Mike popped the top off the can and took a swig. "Ah, ah," he stuttered. "Ah, not really, but I do want to run something past you."

"Shoot." Jethro sat back down on the couch and crossed his ankle over his knee. He noticed Mike was antsy, but couldn't imagine what was making him so nervous. Whatever he had to say, Jethro hoped he wouldn't have to pull it out of him because Mike wasn't much for talking. "Spit it out, Mike. What's on your mind?"

Mike stood and began to pace, not making eye contact with Jethro. "You know Doc Snow, the veterinarian outside of town."

"Yup, I do."

"Well, he's offered me a position in his practice. I've always wanted to be a vet, Gunny, you know that, and this is my chance to learn a trade. He offered me a good salary, too." He glanced at Jethro for a reaction, but there was none. Mike cleared his throat and hurried on. "The Tucker ranch is up for sale, too. I'd like to buy it and bring my family here. What do you think?"

Jethro hunched forward, placing his hands on his knees and weighed his words before speaking. "It's not about what *I* think. Do *you* think you're ready to take all that on?"

Mike had been Jethro's poster boy for response to PTSD treatment at the ranch. His nightmares had all but diminished, he no longer smoked or drank, and he'd worked hard getting it together. He knew Mike missed his family, but this would be quite an undertaking. He wanted to be sure the young Lance Corporal understood all the responsibilities that went with, not only being a husband but a homeowner and a provider as well. Jethro didn't want him to bite off more than he could chew.

Mike sat down again. Bonnie sensed he was anxious and laid her head in his lap, big brown eyes staring up at her master. He began to relax, scratching her behind the ears.

"I'm okay, girl. You can lie down now."

Jethro watched the communication between Mike and Bonnie. It reinforced his decision to use dogs in the recovery of men suffering with PTSD. He smiled, remembering how much Mabel had helped him when his capability to cope with the world was at an all-time low after the death of his fiancée.

"Have you thought this over carefully?" Jethro asked. He knew he couldn't force Mike to stay since he was there voluntarily, but he also didn't want him to fail.

"I have. I've talked to my wife. She's excited about the move."

"Has she ever been to this part of the country?

Mike shook his head.

"If I recall, isn't she from Jersey?"

"She is."

"Montana is a whole different way of life. The winters are unpredictable, we're not close to big cities, and people can seem a bit standoffish at first to an outsider."

"What you're saying is true," Mike said, "but I think she'll fall in love with this state like I have. The mountains are beautiful and majestic. Besides that, she's an outdoor girl and will love all the hiking, biking, and skiing."

"Maybe you're right, but why not see what she thinks by having her visit before you make your decision. Better to be safe than sorry. If you're supposed to own Pete's ranch, it'll still be there for you when you're ready."

Mike's face brightened. "Great idea, Gunny. I'll call Mary tonight and talk it over with her. While she's here, I can show her the ranch and hope she'll like it as much as I do."

"Good choice, Mike. The two of you are more than welcome to stay here in my house. I have plenty of room. I'll give you the time off from work while she's visiting so you can show her around."

The two men stood and shook hands. "Thanks, Gunny. I appreciate your advice."

"You're a good man, Mike. I know you'll make the

right decision."

SADIE BUSTLED ABOUT HER kitchen making last minute preparations for the baby shower she was hosting for Meredith. The guests would be arriving in an hour and she wasn't nearly ready. She still needed to frost and decorate the cake, make the punch and set the dining room table. With Sawyer's help, she'd devised a plan to get Meredith to the house after everyone arrived.

Sawyer was in the living room hanging pink, white and blue crepe paper and a banner that read, *WELCOME BABY!* "Sadie," she called. "Come see what you think."

Sadie wiped her hands on her apron and hurried to the other room. She felt frazzled. "Oh, it's perfect, just perfect," she cooed. "You did a great job, sweetie. Do you think you could set the table for me and make the punch?" Sadie was worried. "I don't know if we're going to get done on time."

"Relax. I'll do whatever you need me to do, so don't fret. It'll get done."

Sadie rushed back to the kitchen and began icing the cake.

Sawyer set the table and filled little guest favors in the shape of baby booties with candy mints. She placed a vase with pink, blue, yellow and white carnations in the center of the table. *Beautiful,* she thought, as she stood back assessing her handiwork.

She joined Sadie in the kitchen and began making the punch with equal parts of orange juice, pineapple juice and ginger ale. She poured the mixture into a large punch bowl and added an ice ring with cherries. She took a sip. "This is so good. Want to try some?" she asked Sadie.

"Not now. I'm busy."

Shortly thereafter, Abby Logan arrived followed by Willa Mae, Maddy Tucker, Vivian Brown, Carrie Boone and several other women from town. They were in a jovial mood, carrying colorfully wrapped gifts, excited about the new babies who were due in a couple of months. Anna Morgan, Meredith's mother-in-law, would arrive with the guest of honor.

"Welcome everyone. Sadie will be with you in a few minutes. In the meantime, please put your gifts on the table by the couch. If you'd like, there's non-alcoholic punch on the buffet in the dining room. Then you can have a seat in the living room.

The ladies smiled and chatted while Sawyer went to find Sadie. She was putting the last of the decorations on the cake. "Oh, it's adorable," Sawyer gushed. The two-tiered chocolate cake, covered with vanilla frosting, had a blue and a pink sugar bootie as the topper. Around the sides were tiny blue and pink footprints. "I could have done this differently if Meredith knew the sex of the babies. But, oh no, they want to be surprised, so I guess we will be, too."

"She'll love it. You did a beautiful job. Are we going to call her now?"

Sadie grinned. "I hope we don't make her go into labor." Sadie picked up the phone and dialed the diner.

"Stony Creek Diner."

"Meredith, its Sadie. You need to come quick. It's your grandfather." She tried to sound breathy and hysterical.

"What happened?" Meredith was already pulling on her sweater and beckoning to Anna.

"He's fallen and I can't get him up." Sadie looked at Sawyer and gave her a thumb's up.

"I'll call Dakota to come help."

"Okay. Better bring Anna, too. He's dead weight."

"Don't panic, Sadie," Meredith said. "We'll be right there."

Sadie hung up. She and Sawyer fist bumped each other and went to the living room to tell the others what was transpiring. "It's kind of a dirty trick when she's this far along, but I couldn't think of any other way to make this a surprise. She's so nosy, she figures everything out."

While the women waited for Meredith, they drank punch and chatted about who won the winner-take-all at the bingo hall, Reverend Anderson's Sunday sermon on human imperfection, and the upcoming breakfast at the fire department.

"Here she comes," Sadie said. "You all go into the dining room and close the door. When you hear her voice, come out and yell surprise!"

Meredith barely brought her truck to a halt before jumping out and rushing up the steps, holding onto her swollen belly. Her heart was beating like a trip hammer. She had been praying all the way over that her grandfather wouldn't die. What would they do without him? He couldn't die, yet. He had to meet his new great-grandbabies.

"Anna, hurry," she hollered after her mother-in-law. Meredith opened the door and stopped still in her tracks. She was puzzled noticing the decorated room. And where was her grandfather?

The dining room door swung open and the women piled into the room. "Surprise!" they shouted.

Meredith burst into tears. Sadie rushed over and gave her a big hug. "It's okay, honey."

"Where's Gramps?"

"He's with Dakota, Yuma and your dad over at the ranch."

"He's not hurt?"

"No, silly. I didn't know how to get you out of the diner in the middle of the day, so I came up with this plan. Now come on over here and sit right down." She ushered Meredith across the room and patted a chair.

"I should hate you for this you know," she said to Sadie, sniffling and wiping at her eyes. "You, too, Anna."

"We know, honey. You can pay us back later, but for now, let's get this party started."

For the next couple of hours, the sounds of laughter

emanated from the house. Gifts were opened and admired, games played, and each woman was asked to write down a name for the babies. Meredith wrinkled her nose as she read each one aloud, Frick and Frack, George and Gracie, Tweedle Dee and Tweedle Dum, and Mickey and Minnie to name a few.

"Thanks, girls, but Dakota and I have already picked out our babies names, boy or girl. You'll know when we know." She smiled and rubbed her tummy when the babies gave her a solid kick.

"Okay everyone, time for cake and ice cream in the dining room," Sadie said.

Just then, the front door opened. "Did I hear ice cream?" Charlie said. Behind him were Dakota, Yuma, and Meredith's dad, Dallas.

"Gramps!" Meredith ran across the room and threw herself into Charlie's arms. "I thought you were hurt. I was so scared." She stepped back and looked at him, before punching him gently in the arm. "You were in on this, you old devil. You should be ashamed of yourself. I almost gave birth right there in the diner." She took a breath. "And the rest of you men, all in on it, too." She scowled at her husband. "I'll deal with you later, Dakota."

"I hope so," he said, a sexy smile on his face.

Sawyer stood back and watched the family dynamic. She missed having a family. She admired how much in love Dakota was with his wife and now they were going to have two precious babies. She hoped that one day she would have children of her own.

"Where's that cake and ice cream?" Charlie hollered.

CHAPTER 35

THE MORNING DAWNED BRIGHT and sunny, rousing Sawyer from a deep sleep. Sunlight streamed gently through the room. She turned on her side and pulled a pillow over her head, not ready to get up. She closed her eyes and let her mind wander while Cooper snored softly at her feet.

Her life had changed dramatically since moving to Montana. She was no longer the high-strung deputy from Florida who thought every day might be her last. She was relaxed, had a strong sense of self, and she was in love. Life for Sawyer Mackenzie was good.

Since sleep wouldn't return, she sat up in bed and dangled her feet over the edge. Shivering from the morning autumn coolness, she grabbed her flannel robe from the bottom of the bed and slipped her feet into her L. L. Bean scuffs. She stretched and ruffled her hair with her hands.

Cooper didn't move, but looked up at her with sad eyes. "What's the matter?" she asked the big dog. "Do you want me to stay in bed and cuddle?" He wagged his tail, but didn't attempt to get up.

Sawyer patted his head and padded toward the kitchen to make coffee.

Finally, Coop slid off the edge of the bed like a snake, taking his time to follow her. He went to the back door and barked. Sawyer let him out to do his business.

She began to make a pot of coffee when her cell phone whistled, indicating she had a text. She picked it up and read the message.

Are you up? She smiled. The message was from Jethro.

Are you? She typed back, an impish grin on her face.

LOL…I am now.

What can I do for you?

Don't even get me started.

Being naughty, Sawyer asked, **Are we sexting?**

Are we? LOL

What do you want?

I just wanted to say good morning, until you started with all the sex talk.

Jethro Byrd, I did no such thing!

Oh yes you did ☺

Sawyer could picture him laughing, and she couldn't help but giggle. **Come over for coffee. I just made a pot.**

Look out your kitchen window.

She pulled back the curtains and grinned. Jethro was outside sitting on Domino waving a bag of Wheat Montana donuts. She opened the door. "Okay, you can come in. I'd have to think about it though, if you didn't have those donuts."

Her breath hitched a little watching him slide off his horse, all sexy-like. She hoped she never got tired of wanting him. He walked across the yard, face clean-shaven, crystal-blue eyes boring holes into her. His blue-plaid shirt hugged his lean, but muscular physique, and his faded blue jeans hugged the rest of him in all the right places. She was nearly breathless by the time he entered the kitchen.

Before he had time to set the donuts on the table, Sawyer wrapped her arms around him and hugged him tightly. She ran her hands through his salt n' pepper hair and breathed in the scent of him, all leather and horses. She raised her head for a kiss and he was happy to oblige, his kiss slow and deliberate. She felt his need for her grow which was an incredibly heady feeling.

Suddenly, Cooper and Mabel began barking and a loud sound was coming from the pasture. "Is that the alpacas?" she asked, but Jethro was already out the door. Sawyer ran after him. Maybe a coyote had gotten into the pen. Something was going on because the whole herd seemed anxious. They were all humming and moving around.

The girls were pacing near Gracie, secured in the "nursery" area of the pasture during her last month of gestation. She was lying down, humming, and in obvious distress.

Jethro assessed the situation and knelt beside her. "It's gonna' be okay, Gracie. We'll get that baby out for you," he said, patting her head.

"What can I do?" Sawyer asked. "What's wrong with her?"

"She has dystocia and needs help delivering the Cria. See that?" He pointed at the impending birth. "The head and one leg are out, but there should be two."

Gracie moved trying to reposition the baby, but there was no change.

Jethro rolled up his shirtsleeves and prepared to help her deliver. "Get me some towels," he told Sawyer.

She raced to the house while Jethro went to work. He pushed the Cria back slightly so as not to tear the uterus, and then felt for the other leg. "Ah, there it is," he said, carefully pulling it out.

"Did I miss anything?" Sawyer asked, handing the towels to Jethro.

He shook his head. "She'll deliver in the next five minutes or so."

With the baby in its proper position, Gracie stood up and continued the birth with no help. The little Cria made squeaks or baby humming sounds, while still hanging out of its mother. Sawyer was in awe. "Did you hear that?" she asked. Tears welled up in her eyes at this precious event.

Jethro took the towel and wiped the nose free from mucus. Gracie made one last push and the little one slid out and onto the ground. Mom turned around and sniffed her baby from head to foot, while it attempted to stand on its wobbly legs.

Millie and her baby, Ally, pasture mates with Gracie, took turns sniffing the Cria. Their curiosity satisfied, they went back to grazing, letting mother and baby bond.

Jethro stood back, a huge grin on his face, and looked at Sawyer who was bawling like an orphaned calf. He put his arms around her and held her close. "That was something special, wasn't it?"

"It sure was. I've never witnessed anything like it in my whole life."

"We've got us a little brown girl this time. She's going to be beautiful."

"She's the same color as cinnamon," Sawyer said. "That would be a great name for her. What do you think?"

"Then, Cinnamon it is." He hugged her again and smiled. "Hey, I have an idea. Why don't you get dressed, we'll have a cup of coffee and a donut, and then we'll take a ride out on the property. It's a gorgeous day."

"But you have your horse here and I can't ride."

"Well, I've been meaning to talk to you about that, little lady." He continued to walk toward the house. "If you're going to be a rancher's wife, you're going to have to learn to ride a horse."

"I'm still afraid of them…wait…what did you just say?" Her eyes were wide with surprise as she grabbed his arm and turned him to look at her. "Say it again." Sawyer's heart skipped and butterflies danced all through her belly.

"I said," Jethro's eyes danced with amusement from the look on her face, "if you're going to be a rancher's wife, then you're going to have to learn to ride. You do plan on making an honest man out of me, don't you?"

Sawyer shrieked and jumped into his arms, wrapping

her legs around his waist and hugging him tightly around his neck. She leaned back and looked into his eyes. "Oh yah, baby. You know it."

"Is that a yes?" He'd been terrified it was too soon, but he loved this feisty redhead and wanted to spend the rest of his life with her.

"It's most definitely a yes."

"I love you, Mac" he said, and kissed her with a slow and gentle tenderness that made her toes curl.

"I love you more, Jethro," and she kissed him right back.

ABOUT THE AUTHOR

Sharon Allen is a native of Maine. She and her husband, Gordon (Bud) moved to Florida in 2005. They reside in the active retirement community, The Villages.

Sharon and Bud were high school steadies, but went their separate ways. They reconnected forty-five years later and were married. They will celebrate their 12th anniversary in November.

Between them, they have six adult children, six adult grandchildren, and three great-grandchildren.

Sharon is a member of the Red Hat Society and is Queen of her chapter, The Sunset Pointer Sisters. She belongs to the Florida Writers Association, Writers League of the Villages, The Write Corner, and Romance Writers of America. She loves to dabble in photography.

For more information about Sharon, visit her website at www. Sharonlallen.net.

35124368R00132

Made in the USA
Charleston, SC
28 October 2014